OSSIE

Acknowledgements

My thanks to all the people who have helped me and guided me in my life and my career especially Mum, Dad, Uncles Bob and George, Tommy Docherty, Dave Sexton, and Lawrie McMenemy, Rose, and my three sons and Lynn.

Thanks also to Andy Mac and Alan Delaprelle for specific help with the book.

Peter Osgood
October 2002

KING OF STAMFORD BRIDGE

PETER OSGOOD
WITH MARTIN KING AND MARTIN KNIGHT

MAINSTREAM
PUBLISHING

EDINBURGH AND LONDON

First published in Great Britain in 2002 by
MAINSTREAM PUBLISHING COMPANY (EDINBURGH) LTD
7 Albany Street
Edinburgh EH1 3UG

ISBN 1 84018 653 4

A catalogue record for this book is available from the British Library

Typeset in Giovanni Book and Trade Gothic

Printed in Great Britain by
Creative Print and Design Wales

Contents

1

Born is the King of Stamford Bridge

> Osgood, Osgood,
> Osgood, Osgood,
> Born is the King of Stamford Bridge.
> *Football chant, adapted from 'The First*
> *Noel' carol c. 1969*

I AM A PAGAN GOD. YOU DON'T BELIEVE ME? OKAY THEN, I AM THE KING. THE King of Stamford Bridge, that is. Or I was. My journey took me from the rolling fields of Berkshire to the epicentre of the Swinging '60s – the Kings Road and Stamford Bridge, home of Chelsea Football Club. It continued (via Mexico) on to Southampton, where an FA Cup was lifted to match the one I had helped win at Chelsea, and America, before I came back to England and eventually down to earth with a jolt. My reign was over.

The journey has been one of adventure, laughter, some tremendous highs and some heart-rending lows. Some of my exploits may be worthy of a pagan, who knows? This is the story of a country lad that could play a bit of football and happened to join a club that happened to become the one most associated with the era of mini-skirts and Mini Minors, Georgy Girl and Georgie Best, and kinky boots and kinky sex. They called it the Swinging '60s – we really got into our stride in the early '70s, but let's not allow a small detail to get in the way.

The name Osgood is Norman or Saxon in origin, depending on whom you believe, and means a god, or pagan god. Pagan means heathen, or not subscribing to one of the leading religions – something I don't do either. Osgoods were mainly yeomen (country people who owned and farmed a modest piece of land) in the past and were well represented in the southern counties of England (especially Wiltshire, Berkshire and Hampshire) for many centuries. In the days before the Industrial Revolution these humble but hardworking people were often referred to as the backbone of England. Us modern Osgoods kept the tradition going, we too had a small piece of land – the back garden of our council house in the village of Dedworth, near Windsor in Berkshire.

Dedworth was once a rural village that became swollen over the last century by the overspill of neighbouring Windsor and the growth of Slough. One of Britain's so-called new towns, Slough was immortalised by John Betjeman in a poem where he invited friendly bombs to drop on the place, and is famous for being the English home of the Mars Bar – production began there in 1932. Although host to some large council estates, Dedworth still retained its country character when I lived there, although locals had an affectionate nickname for the place – Dead Rough. It is said that the last wolf in England was seen or killed in the woods around the village, and Dedworth has many references to this in the names of streets, pubs and suchlike. In my day older folk still spoke with a country twang and one or two of them claimed to have slaughtered the wolf, but maybe that was the cider talking.

In many ways life had changed little in centuries. Even neighbouring Windsor, home to some old bird who lived in a castle, was reasonably tranquil and rustic. I can remember shopping once with Mum when a police car flew past with its siren blaring and blue light flashing. All the shoppers put their bags down on the pavement and turned to watch the spectacle, emergency vehicles in action being such a rarity then. Nowadays we wouldn't bat an eyelid unless, of course, the vehicle happened to knock you down on the zebra crossing in its haste.

I came along on 20 February 1947, born to Les and Ivy Osgood. My stepbrother Mick Ashley had already been around for some four years and was the product of my mum's first marriage which, like many, did not survive the war. My sister Mandy completed the family four years later. Dad was a bricklayer and Mum worked in small-time catering for pubs and hotels. Evidence of the war was still very much around. Rationing continued a good while after I was born. In 1947 the country suffered its coldest winter in the twentieth century so far and the economy was spluttering to a halt. Conditions were becoming more austere, not less, as the general public had expected when peacetime returned. Our royal neighbour Queen Elizabeth II married Prince Philip in the year of my birth, and down at Wembley Charlton Athletic won the FA Cup and Liverpool took the Football League.

My first school was Clewer Green and I stayed there until I was 11 years old. It was a lovely school, but my time there was unremarkable, although it was there that I first took an interest in football. Once I did, I lost all interest in lessons. To me they were the boring interludes between being able to get out into the playground, break into two teams and play wonderful games of football. It's preposterous, but I still remember some of those tarmac contests as well as I do professional ones at the highest level. Wrong-footing goalies. Back-heeling over the line. Flinging myself forward to head home. Very early on I realised that football was something I was good at, and that if you were good at it other people appeared to like and admire you. You were awarded an automatic status that you didn't have to work for, which was handy. I didn't have to beat anyone up or rescue a drowning dog – once I started to shine at football the other boys sort of deferred to me. I don't ever remember working at my skill, just feeling comfortable with a ball and playing, playing, playing at every opportunity.

My brother was an Arsenal fan, so like you do I adopted them as my club. I was a Gooner. Or was it Gunner in those days? Like kids all over the country I took *Charles Buchan's Football Monthly*, ripped out the colour pictures of the players and teams and pasted them on the wall next to my bed. Those specific images are embedded in my mind. The players were boys really, but they looked like middle-aged men to me with their side-partings and short Brylcreemed hair, V-necked football shirts, fixed smiles and squatting poses. George Eastham smiled down at me like a benevolent grandfather from my bedroom wall. I even made it to Highbury on a few occasions. Arsenal were not the force they had been (although they were to be again) but I saw Wolverhampton Wanderers, with Billy Wright, the most revered footballer in Britain at the time, as well as Manchester United's Bobby Charlton (with hair!) and a cheeky young goalscorer at Chelsea by the name of Jimmy Greaves.

Dad built a brick wall in the garden for me to hone my skills against. It is amazing how much enjoyment a boy, a ball and a wall can have. I pounded the ball against it every spare minute, making up fantasies and games in my head, trying to outwit the wall, but it was always solid and dependable. It never crossed my mind that I really could become a professional footballer or play on the same field as Greaves and Charlton. I knew I was good, but then so were a number of boys at the school. I imagined that to be able to become a footballer you had to be 'good' in a way that was beyond my comprehension. I was fairly big for my age and by seven or eight I had got myself into the school team, playing alongside 11 year olds.

Mum and Dad started to take notice and one Christmas they bought me my first pair of football boots. We were far from rich, though I never thought of us as a poor family, but Mum and Dad made Christmas a wonderful time for us all. We'd help Dad put up the Christmas decorations and we were spoilt for love, food and presents. Simple pleasures. Going back to the boots – I loved them so much I wore them around the house, down the shops, anywhere, and refused to take them off until I went to bed at night. Another time they got me a leather football for my birthday and I was equally in love with that. I'd also save up my pocket money and buy the new plastic balls that were coming out, and when I inevitably lost them in someone's garden or they burst I would wander down to the local park and watch the grown-ups playing tennis on the courts. When they hit a ball badly and it flew over the fence, I'd run to fetch it. They'd wait expectantly for the nice boy to throw it back over the wire netting to them, and then look at each other incredulously as I ran as fast as I could in the other direction with the ball. On the occasions I got caught for pranks like this I would plead with Mum for Dad to punish me instead of her. She was one of 12 kids, a local girl. She had forearms like Popeye and if you took a whack off the old girl you knew it. Also like Popeye, she smoked, but fortunately for my street cred it was not a pipe but non-tipped Weights.

Us boys played out on a patch of grass between our houses. We called ourselves the Kenton Lane Boys, which was not particularly imaginative as most of us lived in Kenton Lane, me at number 64, and all of us were boys. Sometimes older kids came over from nearby estates and took us on but invariably we'd beat them. You see, we played together every day and knew each other's game inside out. Imagine how good the England team could be if they played together competitively every day. Tired, but good.

By the age of ten I had graduated to captain of the school team even though I was still one of the youngest members. Around that time I started to notice something else for the first time: girls. And they were showing an interest in me. What was to prove my other great passion was awakening inside me.

One Sunday the family went down to the seaside at Littlehampton. Dad had his trousers rolled up to his knees and sucked on a cigarette; Mum had laid a small tartan blanket out on the beach and had unpacked a picnic. We all sat and stared out at the sea. That was enough for people then. I became a bit restless and spotted four or five boys kicking a football around in the distance. 'Dad, I'm going to go and ask them boys for a game,' I said. We often did that in those days – approach complete strangers and join in their matches. I'm not sure it happens today. You'd probably be accused of trying to steal their valuables, or being a homosexual. Anyway, I joined in and as the afternoon progressed more and more boys, teenagers and men joined the fray. It was fantastic and topped up at about 20 a side. No referee, no colours and jumpers for goalposts. When the goalkeepers got bored they suddenly declared they were 'rush goalies' and dashed up the pitch in the hope of a piece of glory. A crowd had formed too, including Dad, who was deep in conversation with another man. Unfortunately there are no record books to refer to on this one, but the score would have ended up something like 27 each and I reckon I notched up about 12 of the goals for my side. Mind you, the match did last for over three hours.

'Son,' said Dad afterwards, 'that man I was talking to seemed to know a lot about football.'

'Did he?'

'Yes, he said you had everything needed to become a professional footballer. He said, for your age, you were the best forward he has ever seen.'

Dad seemed to be building up to something. Had I been discovered? By a scout from Portsmouth, perhaps? I could barely contain my excitement.

'Who was he then, Dad?'

'No idea.'

Confirmation of my talent seemed to come a few weeks later when I was picked to play for Windsor schoolboys and was pitted against the best from neighbouring counties. There was no doubt that this was a different class of football, but although I didn't set the world alight, I held my own. I still didn't believe that a footballing career beckoned. My dad was a decent player and my uncle played serious non-league football for Windsor & Eton – good players were not rare around our parts.

The obsession with playing football was taking its toll on my schoolwork, though. I simply did not pay any attention in lessons and started to get into a few scrapes with the teachers. Tame stuff by today's standards, when teachers get stabbed and then sued by the pupil for blunting their knives, but at that time even the pettiest incidents took on huge proportions. A mate and me used to climb in a window into the school after everyone had left and steal biscuits from the staff room – I'm not sure why we did this, we certainly were not hungry. It was just the buzz of doing something naughty; a buzz that I'd seek time and time again in my life. Naturally, we eventually got caught. Another time I lost my dinner money on the way to school and when I realised I had made myself late looking for it I played truant. Playing truant is not much fun on your own, so I eventually rolled up at school, but to my horror they punished me by not allowing me to play for the school team. Talk about hitting a boy where it hurts. I was devastated.

Still, my days at Clewer Green were drawing to a close and I sat the exam that more or less decided your entire future then – the famous eleven-plus. If you passed you went to grammar school, and unless you completely mucked up you'd leave five or six years later with a bunch of 'O' and 'A' levels under your arm and a white-collar career to look forward to. If you really excelled you might make university and really become something. A boy from my mum's school became a doctor! How about that? But if you failed you went to a Secondary Modern, where they seemed very keen to interest you in woodwork and metalwork and generally prepared their pupils for blue-collar and manual work. One hundred and forty months on the planet and your life is mapped out forever by a 90-minute test of memory. Yes, you've guessed it, I failed.

Like most Kenton Lane boys I joined Dedworth Secondary Modern, a new school opening up its doors for the first time. It was 1958, the year of the Munich Air Disaster, when the cream of Manchester United's young side were wiped out in a plane crash. It was massive news at the time and the country was united in its mourning. The Busby Babes, as they were nicknamed, were on everybody's minds and even those who had no interest in football were willing the young players that survived and Matt Busby the manager to recover from their injuries and pull through. A few years later the Aberfan disaster would have the same effect nationally as we watched in horror the effects of a landslide devastating a small Welsh mining village.

Dedworth Secondary Modern was livelier than Clewer Green. Besides football they played cricket, tennis and basketball and I competed in all of them. Very quickly I broke into the school football team and soon I was captain again, so I was delighted. We had a great side and as 11 and 12 year olds we were taking on and often beating teams with players near to school-leaving age. I had grown quite tall by now but had managed to retain and hone the first touch and close ball control skills that I had developed as a smaller boy. It was an exhilarating time. I even started doing a bit better academically, especially in maths. For the first time, in this subject at least, I was finishing top of the class too.

In that school team with me was my Uncle Kenny (who was only a year older than me) and my cousin Ray Osgood. The school tough nut was a boy called Ray Moss, but I managed to keep out of his way and generally avoided fights. My excess energy and teenage aggression was being comfortably expended on the football field. Ray Dorey was another fellow pupil. The year 1970 was destined to be a good year for me, and also for Ray: that year I heard of him again – he was at number one in the pop charts with his band Edison Lighthouse and their catchy song 'Love Grows Where My Rosemary Goes'.

I was thrilled when I was selected to play for the Slough and District team. A player called Alan Wilks, who at that point was the best player I had ever come across, bowled me over in that match. I just marvelled at the way he ghosted past defenders and his intricate footwork on the ball. He seemed to me to have a balance and poise that Rudolf Nureyev would have been proud of. It didn't surprise me at all to run into Alan later in my career, firstly at Chelsea and then later playing against him in the Queens Park Rangers team. That first time, though, I was sure he was the next Johnny Haynes and would probably go on to captain England. In later life I often wondered why some players made it and others didn't. There were footballers in my day and even now who couldn't hold a candle to some of the people I played alongside as a kid, yet for some reason they disappeared whilst others who had less talent and flair flourished in the professional game. Maybe it was down to commitment. Maybe luck. A few years later when I was at Chelsea a brilliant young player by the name of Alan Hudson burst into the first team. If you didn't see him play, take it from me, he was one of the best. Ever. He was a born and bred Chelsea lad and if I heard it once I heard it 100 times from the locals: 'Pete, if you think he's good you should see his brother!'

But all good things come to an end. The school team were playing away to a neighbouring school and one kid on our side was particularly gobby. During the game he didn't stop shouting, swearing and generally giving stick, not only to our opponents, but to us as well. You always get one. The kid down the park who roars 'Man on!' at you, as if you didn't know, or appeals to the referee 'C'mon ref!', but of course it's a park game and there is no ref. After the game, which I think we lost, we'd all had enough of this idiot so we tied him up and left him in the changing-rooms. Mr McGowan our headmaster, who was also a Justice of the Peace (which tells you a bit about his attitude towards discipline) did not see the funny side and banned me and a couple of others from playing in the school team.

All was not lost. I had joined the Spital Youth Club by then and was getting a better class of football with the club's team, run by two fine men – Les Marks and Pat Moore. The country was becoming very worried at this time about teenagers' behaviour, and youth clubs had sprung up across the country in an effort to keep them occupied and off the mean streets. A couple of years before, a film called *Blackboard Jungle* starring Glenn Ford as an embattled teacher had introduced a song called 'Rock Around the Clock', and the Teddy Boy was born. The papers would have had you believe that teenagers across the country were beating each other to death with coshes or ripping up cinema seats. I don't recall any such activity in Dedworth, or even Windsor, but how would I have known? My mates and me were too busy out in the woods catching rabbits. We'd take our ferret and head out into the fields and find a used rabbit warren – the giveaway being the fresh droppings in the vicinity. Then we would cover all the boltholes with nets and send our ferret in. Sure enough, the bunnies would come hurtling out and we'd dispatch them quickly and take them home for the pot. That was the theory. It didn't always work out that way. Sometimes no rabbits appeared, and sometimes no ferret. When that happened we'd dig furiously away at the warren to retrieve our animal, but absolutely no sign. One of life's mysteries. Perhaps two rabbits had trapped it in a pincer movement and devoured before plopping out into our nets.

If the youth club people wanted to keep us off the streets and prevent us having flick-knife battles outside Windsor Castle, when really we were trudging around woods with an old ferret in a sack, that was fine with us. We were happy as sand boys, because the club gave us the opportunity to pose in front of the girls and vice versa. In one corner two boys would be sharing a broken cue to play a game of snooker and in another a half-hearted table tennis match would be taking place over a faded green table with a frayed and collapsed net across it. A borrowed gramophone would be emitting the tinny sound of the Everly Brothers for everyone to tap their feet to. A gaggle of girls would be huddled around the coffee counter, giggling and looking over at us. We'd be slouched up against the walls, chewing A–Z gum and feigning disinterest. Every few minutes the comb would be out to ensure the hairdo was still looking good. Some of the girls seemed interested in going beyond a bit of flirting, and all of us boys would have liked to have obliged but the problem was, despite the stories we told each other, none of us knew where to start.

I first realised that Peter had a special talent when he played his first full game for Windsor Corinthians. I wrote to Chelsea about him and they decided to take a look, at the same time a few other clubs were beginning to show an interest. I felt strongly that Chelsea and Peter fitted together well and steered him in that direction. It was like a dream come true when Peter broke through.

After the 1966 World Cup final I was invited to the premiere of a film documentary about the tournament and found myself sitting next to a scout from Queens Park Rangers. We got chatting and he told me that he had looked at Peter a dozen times and could not really see anything in him. I took off my glasses and handed them to the man. 'If you're going to watch the film mate I think you'll need these,' I said.

R. Snashall, Scout and Uncle

2

Life is What Happens to you When you're Busy Making Other Plans

'Beautiful Boy'
John Lennon, 1980

IN 1962, AT THE AGE OF 15, I LEFT DEDWORTH SCHOOL. I HAD NO NERVES OR qualms about what I would do or what life held in store. I've never been one to worry unduly or fret over what hasn't happened yet, and I was quite content to let life happen to me rather than do anything to influence the course of events. Down the youth club a dance called the Twist was all the rage. I was taking more and more notice of the girls and this particular dance, where they wiggled their bums in a very suggestive way, played havoc with my hormones. I had taken to pinching my brother Mick's suit and wearing it out on Friday nights in an effort to look older and smarter. In the wider world Brazil had won the World Cup in the summer, knocking England out in the quarter-finals, and Elvis Presley was number one in the charts with 'Good Luck Charm'. As I write this in 2002, Brazil have won the World Cup, knocking England out in the quarter-finals, and Elvis Presley is once again number one in the charts. Everything changes and nothing changes.

Tony Briner was my inside-forward partner and pal. He was scoring as many goals as I was for Spital. He and I applied together, off our own backs, for a trial with Reading, then a Third Division (South) side. We could barely contain our excitement when we got a letter from Harry Johnston the manager inviting us to Palmer Park for a trial. Harry had been a top player; in fact he was one of the first Players of the Year in 1951 and had forged a great attacking partnership with

Stanley Matthews at Blackpool. The FA Cup final when that Blackpool side featuring Matthews, Stan Mortensen and Harry Johnston defeated Bolton Wanderers 4–3 is one of the most famous ever, and when I was a kid the goals were often reprised in the Pathe News clips at our local cinema. The match is famously known as the Matthews final.

Johnston had also been capped for England during the 1950s, so this was the first time we would present ourselves in front of someone of real standing in the game. With another pal, Jeff White, we set off for Palmer Park. On arrival we were disappointed to learn that Harry Johnston was not even there to welcome or watch us. Apparently he was off scouting so we wouldn't even have the consolation of meeting a famous ex-England player when we were rejected. The junior side were training and there were a few other boys like us apprehensively standing around. A couple of club officials ticked our names off on a clipboard and told us to get changed and join in the loose match that was being played in front of us. It all seemed very disorganised and informal. Still, I played okay and managed to score twice, but had still not recovered from the blow that the manager himself was not there to see me. When the game ended we lingered awhile like spare pricks at a wedding, but no one approached us so we slouched off to rejoin Jeff, who had been watching from the touch-line. I'm not sure if Jeff was just trying to make me feel better, but he said that one of the club officials had made some positive comments about my game.

'He said, tell your friend Osgood we'll be giving him a ring,' finished Jeff.

'They'll have a hard bloody job. We're not on the phone.'

Shortly after that Harry Johnston left his job at Reading and I was pleased. Funny how you can take a dislike to someone you have never met. Incidentally, Roy Bentley, the centre-forward hero of Chelsea's 1955 league-winning side, replaced him as manager. Chelsea fans need no reminding that 1955 was and at present remains the only time Chelsea have been league champions. Roy remained at Reading for some years.

Around this time, along with Uncle Ken, we were selected to play football for Berkshire at Reading's Elm Park ground. In our part of the world this was the equivalent of playing at Wembley. A real ground, with real spectators, floodlights, match officials – the lot. I was playing particularly well at the time, generally knocking in between 36 and 40 goals a season. Les Marks, the secretary of Spital, decided to write off to Arsenal and suggest they come and see me. Les never mentioned this to me, I suspect because if he did and they didn't respond he figured I'd be disappointed and it might affect my game. Arsenal did respond, though, and sent a form for me to fill in setting up a trial. Les was thrilled.

'Peter, Peter,' he said, waving the form under my nose, 'they want you for a trial, son. Arsenal want you to go up for a trial.'

I studied the form for a minute or two, smiled and then ripped it up.

'What are you playing at?' Les implored.

'I can't go to Arsenal for a trial!' I exclaimed, thinking of all their big stars, that packed ground and their illustrious history. 'It'd be wasting their time and I'd make myself look a prize pillock!'

Les shook his head, but I was not for being talked round. I suppose at the back of my mind I could picture myself breaking into Windsor & Eton, or really scaling the heights and making the squad of a lower division league side, but Arsenal, the Gunners of Highbury – that was ridiculous. Also, I was not the best player in the Spital side and I had seen some of the other boys traipse off for trials at lesser clubs and come back unsuccessful and downhearted. Bobby Woolfe, one of the other Spital Old Boys, had been for a trial with Crystal Palace but when he bought back the kit none of us fancied going there. Looking back on it, I think one of the reasons I wasn't keen on the trial was that I feared failure, or more accurately couldn't be bothered to risk it. At Spital I was a star – we'd won the Slough Town Cup for God's sake! I didn't fancy going somewhere else and being bottom of the pile again.

My first job was on a trading estate in Slough as a filing clerk for a gun metal firm. I cycled the five miles each day to and from the office and I hated it. Everyone was very kind to me, but sitting in an office placing pieces of paper behind and in front of other pieces of paper did my head in. The six-pound-a-week wages were welcome and not bad for the time. Mum and Dad were pleased that some extra money was coming into the family coffers, but they knew that I was not really happy and was itching for something else. Problem was, I didn't know what. Six months later I moved to a washing-machine factory in Eton, where I was a sort of spare-hand, and I felt a little more useful but not much. Really I wanted to work out of doors. Granddad had been a plasterer and my brother and Dad were both bricklayers. I envied them coming in from work with their sun-kissed faces in the summer or ruddy complexions in winter. The brick dust on their clothes was proof if you needed it of a good day's work. When I worked at the factory and returned home to my family in the evening, I felt almost a fraud among working men. I don't think Dad wanted me to go on site, believing that an office career was preferable in the modern age to a manual one, but he was supportive when I told him I wanted to swap my washing-machine spanner for a trowel. I got a start with Dad as an apprentice bricklayer at F.J. Lane & Sons of Windsor and couldn't have had a better teacher.

A stunning girl called Irene Kelly became my first girlfriend. We played tennis together, among other things. Tennis really brings out the best in women I find. But girlfriend or no girlfriend, football was taking up most of my time. I was playing for Spital Old Boys on a Saturday and Windsor Corinthians on a Sunday, and even though I was out at work and supposedly above all that I still turned out of a summer's evening on the patch of grass with the Kenton Lane boys. I managed to score 54 goals for Spital in one season, and that was on the top of the 35 my brother Mick Ashley nicked from the right wing. My Uncle Bob played in the Windsor Corinthians and not being a glory-seeker like us other Osgoods, he was content to be a dependable midfielder. Bob was more convinced than I was that I had the ability to make the professional grade and constantly told me so. He wrote off to clubs on my behalf because he knew I would not, and this time he tried Chelsea Football Club. When the letter came, similar to the Arsenal one, because he was my uncle I couldn't duck out of it.

We were to turn up at Hendon one Saturday towards the end of the season. Brother Mick, Spital Club secretary Len Hill and myself set off in Mick's trendy (blue with a white strip) Ford Anglia. I was not at all nervous. The Reading experience had taught me that it would probably be a non-event in any case. On arrival there were about 60 to 100 kids milling around, but this time there was some organisation. It was like the auditions for *Pop Idol* except most of us could probably sing. Us boys were split into groups and would play in four half-hour periods. A man I later learned was Dick Foss and Chelsea's Starfinder General approached.

'You will play in the first two periods, son.'

'That's handy, I've got a cup match this afternoon,' I cheekily replied.

Did I catch a sideways glance as Dick walked off to the next group? Dick Foss, it turned out, was a scout and a half, having at that time discovered for Chelsea Ken Shellito, Terry Venables, Jimmy Greaves, the Harris brothers, Jim McCalliog, John Hollins, John Boyle, Barry

Bridges, Bobby Tambling and Jim Thomson, among others. He had also played professionally for Chelsea before joining the back-room operation.

I scored early on, but did not think I had a particularly good game. Everyone was running themselves into the ground, determined not to let the opportunity pass without giving it their best shot and desperate to catch the club's eye. But I had never played in that way and never would. Some said I was a lazy player and I suppose I was. But I couldn't see the point in chasing balls you knew you would not get just to impress the scout, the manager, your team mates, even the crowd. I believed in keeping fresh and sharp and well positioned for any attacking opportunities that arose. Some people call this goal hanging, I believe. At the end of my stint Dick Foss approached me with a clipboard and passed me a biro. 'Sign there, son.'

I assumed I was signing some sort of expenses or proof of attendance chitty, so I scrawled my name, handed the pen back to Dick and turned to leave.

'You don't seem too happy,' smiled Dick.

'Happy about what?'

'Signing for Chelsea Football Club.'

I was now an amateur footballer attached to Chelsea. In effect this meant that I was not actually playing for Chelsea, or on Chelsea's payroll proper, but I had amateur status and as and when Chelsea wanted me they could have me. It basically stopped other clubs nicking me while they looked at me further and watched how I developed. On the way home in the car we were all elated. We knew it was an important step in the right direction but I, at least, was not under the illusion that it would necessarily lead to a professional footballing career. That afternoon I scored twice in Spital's 3–2 cup win. That was still the real world for me.

Some considerable time later, still curious as to what Dick Foss had seen in me, I asked him.

'You moved well, Ossie,' he explained. 'You hit the ball with both feet instinctively. It was the way you played the ball rather than what you did with it that impressed me. I've seen players with snazzy skills and not been impressed, but I've signed others on the strength of one pass. I've signed lads who have barely touched the ball in their trial but have shown the ability to run off the ball, and took up positions that showed they could read the game. I look for what a player *attempts* to do with the ball. If the ideas are there, coaching can bring them out.'

A week later I got a call to turn up at Fratton Park for a South-east Counties League game for Chelsea Juniors (they call it Youth now I think) against Portsmouth. Again we travelled down in Mick's motor, and when I joined the other apprentices in the dressing-room they all looked up and started laughing. They were dressed to a man in dark blazers and neatly pressed strides. Most had ties. I wore my work jeans and denim jacket. My spirit level was poking out of the top of the plastic shopping bag that I had carried my football boots down in.

'See you're dressed for the occasion,' laughed one lad.

'What do you do for a living – scarecrow?' cackled another cockney wide boy.

But a familiar face was among them, Alan Wilks, the boy I had played for the county with, and I changed into my kit next to him. Another boy nodded over at me and gave me a reassuring smile as if to say, 'Don't worry, they're only joking.' He was Peter Houseman. Johnny Boyle was also in the team. Chelsea won 7–0 and Worzel Gummidge netted a hat trick. I'd have scored more if I hadn't been carried off after an hour with cramp. It was a great feeling to know I had impressed, not only the Chelsea club people but also my team mates.

Shortly after, my career really started to build some momentum. Chelsea were pitted against West Ham United in the Southern Counties Junior Floodlight Cup final. We were captained by John Hollins and led 2–0 from the first leg clash at Stamford Bridge. I had not played in that match and had not expected to; I was still very much the new kid on the block. It was a great result for Chelsea because the young West Ham side they played against was considered invincible, with John Sissons, Harry Rednapp and Martin Britt their big names.

Besides Holly and Peter Houseman, we had a big centre-forward named Eric Whittington in the side. Eric had got those two important goals in the first leg. So it was a great shock to me when Dick Foss picked me for the second leg at Upton Park in place of Eric. For the first time I had some nerves. It was a big, important match at a First Division ground. I had replaced a lad who was doing well and had secured the first leg win. There would be a 10,000 crowd; the largest I had played in front of, and that crowd would include most of my family. I needn't have worried because Chelsea won 3–1 and I put away two of the goals. The second goal was a good header from a corner. Everyone was delighted and Dick Foss lavished me with praise.

I think he was relieved that I had proved his judgement correct. Even Harry Medhurst, the first-team trainer, watched the match and said later: 'From the moment he touched the ball I knew that this lad could be a great player. He reminds me of Charles Buchan.'

I never saw Charles Buchan play, but he published a bloody good magazine (*Charles Buchan's Football Monthly*). At 17 years old I now started to dare to believe that maybe my future life was going to be a little bit different from what I had expected.

The next day on the building site Dad was bubbling over, but for the other brickies, chippies and labourers the Southern Counties Junior Floodlight Cup meant nothing and I kept tight-lipped about it. At lunchtime, though, when we sat down to eat our sandwiches and crack open the thermos flasks, one of the labourers unfolded his *Daily Express* and there was a decent match report with my name in the headline: 'NEW BOY OSGOOD SHINES'. I had to look at it two or three times for it to sink in. Perhaps it was at this point I stopped being Peter Osgood and became *Peter Osgood*.

> If ever my mum could have apportioned the blame for my failing in the school education system to anything or anyone, it would have been Chelsea Football Club and in particular, Peter Osgood.
>
> I became a Chelsea supporter at an early age. By the time I was seven all four walls of my bedroom were covered with pictures of the team, with one wall devoted in its entirety to Ossie. By the time I was in my third year at primary school, my end-of-term reports were punctuated with phrases such as 'He must stop daydreaming about Chelsea' or 'It is important that he realises that there is more to life than Peter Osgood'.
>
> D. Johnstone, Chelsea Supporter

3

Docherty's Diamonds

CHELSEA FOOTBALL CLUB HAD BEEN FORMED IN 1905 BY THE MEARS construction dynasty. Gus and Joe Mears were football fans and were determined to build a stadium in south London even though they didn't have a football club to put in it. Stamford Bridge was constructed alongside the District Underground line on the Fulham Road, parallel with the Kings Road. When completed the stadium was offered to Fulham Football Club, but they declined the invitation. Chelsea Football Club was quickly formed and when admission to the Southern League was denied they joined the Second Division of the Football League. The Mears family remained owners of Chelsea for the next 70-odd years and chairman Brian Mears, grandson of co-founder Joe Mears – and son of the Joe Mears who was still there when I joined (known as Mr Chelsea) – outlasted me, if only for a short while.

Keeping goal for Chelsea in that debut season was William 'Fatty' Foulke, who was certainly Chelsea's first celebrity player and set the mould of out-of-the-ordinary footballers that would personify Chelsea's character over the rest of the century. Some say he weighed 20 stone – not even Tommy Lawrence, Liverpool's keeper in the 1960s, was that fat. By all accounts he was a real character and sadly his life entered a swift decline after his playing days were over. He died at the age of 40 from pneumonia, eking out a living as a seaside novelty act, where holidaymakers were invited to take shots against him on the sand.

The team's achievements were unremarkable for around 50 years after the club was founded as they yo-yoed between the Second and

First Divisions without winning any major honours. In 1915, during the First World War, when attentions were understandably diverted, they did make the FA Cup final but succumbed to Sheffield United by 3–0. Besides a prolific goalscorer, George 'Gatling Gun' Hilsdon, Chelsea could boast few other household names in their first 50 years of existence. In the 1930s a nifty Scottish forward came to the Bridge for a relatively small time. Hughie Gallacher was still talked of when I arrived at Chelsea even though it was 30 years since he had moved on. Hughie too met a sad end, throwing himself under a train after his retirement from football. Tommy Lawton, one of the most famous centre-forwards ever (with one of the most famous centre-partings ever), also spent a bit of time at Chelsea just after the Second World War. Tommy did live into his old age but was beset by financial problems at various times during his retirement.

In 1935 Chelsea witnessed their record attendance. Close to 83,000 people crammed inside Stamford Bridge to witness the visit of Arsenal, the Manchester United of the time. They were reaching peaks that hadn't been attained up until then and have only been surpassed by the Manchester United side of recent years. George Allison was manager and that season he was riding high after achieving a consecutive hat trick of League Championships for the Gunners started by Herbert Chapman who had died the previous year. Remarkably, Chapman had also managed this in the previous decade with Huddersfield Town. Leading that sizzling Arsenal forward line was an Englishman named Ted Drake and it was he that would change Chelsea's on-field fortunes in the 1950s.

When Ted's playing days were finally over he came to Chelsea as manager in 1952 and immediately began moulding the young side that came to be known as 'Drake's Ducklings'. Drake made some inspired signings, including Frank Blunstone from Crewe and Roy Bentley from Newcastle. Ron Greenwood, later to become manager of West Ham United and England, was also in the team. Bentley became captain as well as the side's top scorer and finally led Chelsea to the League Championship in 1955. Still, this was not one of the greatest Championship-winning sides ever, and the title was attained with the lowest-ever amount of points. Nevertheless it is the only one Chelsea has won and therefore it is more than good enough for us. The Chelsea fans revered Roy Bentley and when I first arrived at Stamford Bridge his name was still daubed in graffiti on a wall down by the North Stand end.

Sadly Ted Drake was unable to build on the success of the '55 team and things went downhill steadily. Had it been today Ted would have lost his job almost immediately after winning the Championship, for the following season Chelsea only managed 16th in the league, surely one of the worst showings ever by a Championship-winning team in their defence season. But Joe Mears was neither ungrateful nor short-sighted and Drake kept his job until 1962, when Chelsea were finally relegated from the First Division and Drake was politely fired and replaced by a fiery young Scot who had joined earlier from Arsenal to become his deputy. His name was Tommy Docherty.

Tommy had been disappointed that the club had sold their brilliant young goalscorer Jimmy Greaves to Milan and that Ted Drake had allowed it to happen. In the 1962–63 season, Tommy's first full season as manager, he took Chelsea straight back into the First Division. It was at the tail end of the following season that I signed amateur forms with the club and at the beginning of the 1964–65 campaign I was delighted to be offered terms as a ground-staff boy. This was a big step forward from the amateur status I had held up until then. Chelsea were now paying my wages, this was my full-time job and I would have to take an extended holiday from the building trade, although I kept my tools handy . . . just in case.

If I thought my life was about to become that of a budding young star I was very much mistaken. The training ground was at a place called Welsh Harp and it entailed me catching the 6.30 a.m. brown bus from Dedworth to Windsor BR station, from there to Paddington main line, where I picked up the tube to Kings Cross, then on to Brent and finally another bus ride to Welsh Harp. By the time I arrived each day I was knackered and fed up with all the travelling. The training ground was gruesome and I was shocked that a First Division club would have their players train in such a place. The facilities were . . . missing. Jock, the groundsman, would insist on us all partaking in a cup of tea with him, which he produced from an enormous pot. None of us really fancied this as he had a habit of stirring the pot first with a dirty and multi-coloured old paint-stick.

After training I often had to jump on the coach to Stamford Bridge, where all manner of chores awaited me. On Mondays, if the first team had played at home, it was our task to clean the entire terraces. Every peanut bag, sweet wrapper and fag packet had to be picked up and deposited in rubbish bags. The only consolation to this backbreaking job was you did find a few coins that, naturally, I handed in to the club. Another task was to polish the senior players' boots. We were designated a couple of players each and one of mine was Ken Shellito. By now I had been watching Chelsea as much as I could and I admired Ken enormously. He was a great full-back who had already won an England cap, and if a serious knee injury hadn't hijacked his career I'm sure he would have played in the 1966 World Cup final. Of course, I was now seeing the first team players on a regular basis but as a junior I was not part of their clique. They were decent to us boys, all of them having been in our shoes at one time or another. Even then I could see that although the other players held Ken Shellito in great respect it was Terry Venables, a cheeky cockney boy, who was the guv'nor.

The £10 a week I was being paid was more than I had been getting in the office or on the site. Chelsea also reimbursed my expenses, which was a godsend considering all the transport fares I was clocking up. However, what I liked best was the club blazer that I was given. Like the football boots all those Christmases ago, it was hard for me not to wear it all the time, though I can't remember if I had it on the day I went to Agar's Plough, an annual funfair held on the playing fields of Eton College. They say that some of England's most glorious military victories were planned on the playing fields of Eton. I don't know about that, but it was there that I met my wife. I was due to go with Jeff White, but he let me down so I decided to go on my own. I spotted a really pretty young girl with shiny black hair and a cute smile standing with some friends around a stall. She must have smiled at me, because although I had some front in those days, I can't believe I would have risked just bowling over and chatting her up unless I had, or thought I had, some sign of encouragement. Her name was Rose Snow and I asked her out. She lived in Winkfield and worked in the Lloyds Bank opposite Windsor Castle. It's still there and hasn't been converted into a Wetherspoon's yet. We arranged to go to the local picture house the next week. It's a compliment to Rose, I hope, that I cannot remember which film we went to see. I was besotted by her and am sure I was paying no attention to what was on the big screen in front of me.

We courted (as it was politely known in those days) and I was just so happy with my lot. Rose and I were both young and it was a good time to be a teenager. The Beatles and the Rolling Stones had burst onto the music scene and suddenly being a teenager and 'trendy' was 'where it was at'. Although Elvis and the rock 'n' roll movement are normally attributed with galvanising the younger generation, I believe it was only in the '60s that society actually realised youth culture was here to stay and that young people had influence and power. It sounds far-fetched from today's perspective but back in the '50s and early '60s no one took you seriously until you were hitting 30, and you really didn't know that you had had your youth until it was too late. A boy was wearing his short trousers, snake belt and Tuf shoes one minute and the next, before he knew it he was sunk down in the armchair wrapped in his woollen cardigan, smoking his pipe, in front of the telly watching *Whickers World*. Once John Lennon, Mick Jagger, Pete Townshend and the rest of them had arrived nothing was ever going to be the same again.

After a few weeks Rose took me home to Winkfield to meet her mum and dad. Martha, her mother, was a formidable Welsh woman and Eric, her father, fortunately for me was a football fanatic and any apprehension I had soon dissolved in long conversations about the game. Rose actually lived next door to her parents with her nan and granddad, Violet and Lionel, who were a marvellous old couple. Due to the restrictions on space in her parents' place Rose had lived in her grandparents' house from an early age, but it didn't matter who lived where; they were one big happy family.

We were kids really, me and Rose, but the problem with kids is that when they reach a certain age they have adult impulses and being very much in love, Rose and I were no different. We had a sex life of sorts, snatching moments of intimacy where we could, but I was not prepared at all when Rose told me calmly that she was in the club. And we're not talking Chelsea Football Club here. Unplanned pregnancies were a running theme on the big screen at the time with a new breed of gritty British films like *Alfie* and *A Taste of Honey* dealing with the subject. So whilst the country as a whole was beginning to admit such things did happen, I was proving it beyond doubt. In a way I already had experience of such things. Excuse me if I slip into '60s speak here: brother Mick had recently *got his girlfriend into trouble* and had *done the decent thing* and married his girl. However, Mick was 4 years older than me and the difference between 21 and 17 years of age is a yawning chasm in terms of maturity, so I was not sure how Mum would react when I broke the news. She was scrubbing the oven with a Brillo pad at the time.

'Mum, Rose has got pregnant,' I announced.

She slid backwards on her knees across the lino and lifted her head out of the oven.

'Rose got herself pregnant did she? You had nothing to do with it then?'

I smiled weakly. 'What shall I do Mum?'

'You'll marry her, thats what you'll do,' Mum replied sternly.

I knew what she was thinking. First Mick and now me. Stupid boys. Just when some money was coming in to the house at long last, too.

Tommy Docherty was beginning to make a name for himself at Chelsea. Always ready with a quote, the press warmed to him. The exciting team he had moulded was dubbed by the press 'Docherty's Diamonds' and great things were expected of it. I'd seen Tommy around the club, but besides a cursory nod here and there we'd had no real contact. The first time I became aware that he knew I existed was after a youth match against a Scottish team called Drumchapel Amateurs. I scored 6 in our 9–2 victory and in a newspaper article Tommy was said to be taking delight in the disappointment of one of the Scottish selectors who was watching the game when he discovered that young Osgood was not a Scot.

Shortly after that game I was elevated to the reserves for the first time. The step up in class was not as great as I had expected. Nevertheless it was a slick operation with many good players in the team: I played against John Radford and Ray Kennedy, who would later become part of Arsenal's Double-winning side, and alongside Frank Upton, Joe Fascione, Allan Harris (older brother of Ron) and Jim McCalliog, to name just a handful.

As a reserve I was now no longer under the protective wing of Dick Foss and his assistant Dick Spence. They may have been a pair of Dicks, but they were a great team and discovered and nurtured so much talent for Chelsea. Spence had been a useful winger for Chelsea in the '30s and had played for England twice. He was very modest about his achievements. I was upset and absolutely baffled when Tommy got rid of Dick Foss some time later. But as a reserve we all came under the coaching supervision of a square-jawed, determined man. His name was Dave Sexton and our lives were to be entwined for many years to come.

After scoring two goals in my reserve team debut my confidence was growing. I now believed that I was going to make it. Many of the reserve team players were on their way in or on their way out of the first team and as I said, I did not find the step up in class daunting in the slightest, except on one or two occasions. One game was against Cardiff City and the centre-half that was marking me looked older than my dad. Possibly he was. I thought that I would be able to run rings around this decrepit old sod, but it was not to be. He beat me every time, on the ground and in the air. Frankly he made a monkey of me. Frank Upton and Allan Harris slaughtered me afterwards. 'You were useless, Osgood,' they spat. And they kept on and on. We hadn't even lost – it was a 0–0 draw. Finally, just as I was about to burst into tears, Barry Gould (whose brother Ian was a Sussex cricketer) jumped to my defence. 'Leave him alone, you two! He's a kid of 17. That John Charles may be near the end of his career but he's still one of the best players that ever walked on a pitch.' John Charles. I knew the name but little else. That night I asked my dad and he told me that John Charles was the greatest Welsh footballer that ever lived. He was gobsmacked that I had just played against him.

When I was picked to play for England Under-18 youth side in Germany and we lost to the East Germans 3–2 in the final, I got on the score sheet and was voted Player of the Tournament. I was positively bristling. With my confidence growing, and mindful of the fact that I would soon have the responsibility of a child, I decided to go and see the Boss. A few of the first team were out injured, yet I had not been picked to replace them, which rankled me. I was now on £20 a week but felt that I should be earning first team wages even if that meant going to another club. From Placid Pete to Obstreperous Osgood in a few months.

I opened up with 'I want a transfer. If you won't play me in the first team there is obviously no future for me here.'

The Doc let me say my bit, but when he looked up he was like a man possessed. Beads of sweat had broken out on his forehead and a blue vein throbbed angrily over his eyebrow. 'Osgood, you have signed a contract to play for Chelsea. And play for Chelsea you will. You will play in the first team lad, but it will be when I bleeding well decide, not you!'

He was roaring and I feared that I'd gone too far, but as quickly as he erupted he calmed down and we managed to have a good talk. I left the office that day having withdrawn my transfer request (if that is what it was) and the Doc gave me a pay rise, but he made no promises about when he would give me my first team debut.

He had other things on his mind. The first team were up in Blackpool on a Friday night before a league match with Burnley. They were guests of the Norbreck Hotel and Terry Venables, Bert Murray, George Graham and Marvin Hinton, probably bored (for in-room erotic films had not been invented then), had sneaked out of the hotel and hit the town for a bit of a drinking session. The night porter took great delight in grassing them up to Docherty when he returned from his dinner.

'Ridiculous,' Tom sniffed dismissively. 'Bring your keys and we'll check the rooms.'

The night porter was only too pleased to oblige. As he opened the door of the first room and switched on the light he could see a human form in each bed. One weary voice asked, 'What's up Boss?' In the next room the story was the same, but the unforgettable smell of Old Spice had twanged Tom's suspicious bone. He walked over to George Graham's bed and flung back the bedclothes to find George in all his suited finery. The lads had beaten the Doc back to the hotel, but only just. He didn't see the funny side, did his nut and sent eight offenders home. The remaining team, bolstered by some reserves summoned from London, went on to lose 6–2 at Turf Moor and Docherty was not shy in coming forward over where he felt the blame lay. Even I did not escape his wrath. 'Don't think I don't know that if you'd been in Blackpool, you'd have been the ninth one going home,' he breathed at me in menacing tones. This was the first in a series of public incidents involving Chelsea players and drink that continues to this day. More significantly it signalled the end of Tom's relationship with some key players and the break-up of his first Chelsea team. Docherty's Diamonds were not to last forever, it seemed.

When I first saw Ossie play at the training ground I was astounded and ensured we had the boy fully signed up in case anyone tried to pinch him from under our noses. A big, strong lad, he was good in the air and had two good feet. In today's transfer market he'd be worth £30–40m. The only player I could liken him to in the current game is Dennis Bergkamp.

Contrary to all the rubbish that has been printed about Ossie, as far as I am concerned he was a model pro and fiercely loyal. I would go as far as to say he was the greatest English forward of his generation. I love the lad.

T. Docherty, TV and Radio Pundit

4

One Wedding, Two Debuts and a Broken Leg

TOMMY DOCHERTY DID GIVE ME MY FIRST TEAM DEBUT EVENTUALLY, ON 16 December 1964. I was not yet 18; too young to drink in pubs, too young to vote if I was so inclined, but soon to be married and with a child on the way. I had just got dressed after training one afternoon at the Bridge and I glanced nonchalantly at the team sheet pinned up on the wall for the upcoming fifth round League Cup tie at Workington. As usual it started with '1. Bonetti', but as my eye travelled to the bottom of the sheet I was dumbstruck to see 'Osgood'. I was in the pool of players to travel north. I really had no idea that my debut was imminent, however much I thought I deserved it. The team were playing well and at that stage were still in the running for the championship, the FA Cup and the League Cup. It dawned on me that if someone became injured I would be there in the shake-up with them.

Whatever happened to Workington? I know they were not re-elected to the Football League a few years later but I have not heard of the team or indeed the town since. When can you honestly say you have met someone from Workington? Or read about the place in the papers, or heard on the news of something happening there? Perhaps it was only because of the football club that anyone outside of the town had heard of it anyway, and when the club met its demise the town sunk back into anonymity. But there were plenty of people up there when Chelsea visited the then Third Division side. The small ground was packed to the rafters that night. I felt privileged to be sitting in the dugout with Tommy and trainer Harry Medhurst, a real part of things at last. Tommy and Harry were not in tune with my pride though, out on the field little Workington were working the Chelsea stars over. We fought to leave with a 2–2 draw but not until after a nail-biting finale when Workington had a goal disallowed. It was a great experience for me but I hadn't got off the bench.

The day before the replay the Doc beckoned me towards him. 'You're in the team tomorrow night son. Don't worry, play your natural game and you'll be fine. From what I hear you've deserved the chance. Best of luck.' That was one of the best moments of my life; I could have kissed the boss but I tried to stay cool. It was not a throwaway game. The competition was growing in importance; soon the winners would qualify for Europe via the Inter Cities Fairs Cup and victory over Workington would put us in a two-leg semi-final against Aston Villa. I had been with Chelsea ten months.

All my family, my team mates from Spital and many of my friends made the trip from Berkshire to the Bridge for my debut. The team had been told to meet at the Hotel Montana near the ground at 4.30 p.m. for a meal and the team talk. I drove there in the green and white Hillman Minx purchased from my Uncle George. I can remember the number plate, WMO 625, and I can also remember thinking as I parked outside the hotel that I must take my driving test. It wouldn't be good to get a nicking for driving without a licence now I was a first team Chelsea player. I had steak and toast and kept very quiet as the Doc talked tactics. Some of the more senior players joined in the talk, even making suggestions of their own. Terry Venables was particularly vocal. The meal, the hotel and the team talk were a revelation and quite daunting to me. The only thing I asked the whole time was 'Where's the ketchup?'

My nerves increased as we got to the ground and entered the dressing-room. Eight thousand fans were waiting expectantly, most of whom would never have heard of me. All sorts of thoughts swirled around my head. Say I missed an open goal, played terribly? Let all these professionals down? But I didn't allow the nerves to dull the moment of sheer pride and excitement as I pulled on the royal blue Chelsea shirt as a senior player for the first time. Workington were good and for long periods outplayed us, to the frustration and annoyance of the crowd who had assumed their performance up there was due to the home advantage and the 'little club rising to the big occasion' syndrome, and that we would demolish them here at

Stamford Bridge. On their side was a guy called Keith Burtenshaw, who became better known for his stint as manager at Tottenham Hotspur in the 1970s and '80s. We were not looking good and my debut was turning out to be a damp squib.

With nine minutes remaining George Graham glided through the midfield and found me with an intelligent pass on the edge of the area. I slipped through and swerved right past the advancing Workington keeper, and clipped the ball across him and into the back of the net. I had no time to savour the moment because before we knew it Tommy Knox had thumped another shot against the post and I was there to tap it firmly home. We were through and I had arrived. After the game the players and Tommy himself hugged me and ruffled my hair like you do a kid. It was a great feeling and rejoining my family and friends afterwards was even better.

In the morning my local newsagent in Windsor must have thought I was an overgrown paperboy as I waited for him to cut the string on his bundles. I bought every newspaper and rushed home to spread them across the floor and devour them. 'Boy Osgood hits two in Cup debut,' screamed the *Daily Sketch*, 'Wonder Boy of Windsor' exclaimed another. I felt like I was reading about someone else. There have been some fantastic highs in my life but those first days after my debut against long-forgotten Workington were among the best of them.

Although I had grabbed some goals and headlines I was under no illusion that my game had been particularly good. Even I could see that I had a good deal to learn about tactics and formations and therefore it was no surprise when I found myself back in the reserves immediately after the League Cup game. My fellow reserve player John Boyle got picked against Aston Villa in the quarter-final and he too scored in our 3–2 victory at Villa Park. No doubt John was experiencing the same intensity of emotion that I had just been through. He was already displaying an eye for the ladies and his strike rate was pretty damned good. Boylers was dating beauty contest winners when George Best was still tucked up in bed at Mrs Fullaway's house in Manchester reading *The Dandy*. We went on to win a two-leg final against Leicester City. Tommy had earlier signed a dour, tough-looking fellow Scot, Eddie McCreadie, and he played in the first leg at centre-forward. He wasn't to score too many goals in his career at Chelsea because he carved his niche as a full-back soon after, but the winning goal he scored against Leicester in the 3–2 first leg victory was worthy of the best striker in the land. Picking up the ball in his own half he galloped 70 yards, wasting 3 Leicester defenders before forcing it past Gordon Banks in the City goal. The League Cup was a relatively new competition and the fact that only 20,690 spectators witnessed the first match at Stamford Bridge against the 51,000 who had packed in to see Tottenham Hotspur in the previous home league game is a reminder of how seriously it was taken at the time. In the next couple of decades its importance did grow, especially when the finals started to be staged at Wembley. Nevertheless it was a cup, an honour to add to Tommy's promotion from the Second Division.

Rose and I were married at Windsor Registry Office in the shadow of Windsor Castle one Saturday morning. Both families were there, but I had no time to party or celebrate then for I was due to play in a reserve match against Shrewsbury at the Bridge and took the train from Windsor to the match. I scored 3 in a 6–0 win and whilst showering afterwards I mentioned to my team mates that I had to rush because I needed to get back to a Chinese restaurant in Windsor to celebrate my wedding.

'You recently got married then, Os?' asked one.

'Quite recently,' I answered, 'about six hours ago actually.'

It was a good evening and afterwards Rose and I went back to the house in Lovell Road, Winkfield, where we had already been living for a few months. We had decided we'd worry about honeymoons and such things after our little baby was born.

Chelsea finished the season winning the League Cup, reaching the semi-final of the FA Cup and finishing third in the League. Tommy Docherty had rapidly turned around the side that had ended up floundering under Ted Drake and within a couple of seasons had them challenging for all honours. With an undoubted pool of young talent competing for places with the established players there was a buzz around the place. When the campaign was over Tom decided to reward everyone, including me, with a six-week close season tour of Australia. Flattered as I was, and despite being keen to visit an overseas country – at this point I hadn't even made it to the Isle of Wight – I went to see the boss and told him I couldn't go because Rose was pregnant and the baby could be born whilst we were away. Tommy fished in his desk and produced my contract. 'Did you sign this, lad?'

'Yes I did.'

'Well, you're going to Australia then.'

This time I was not going to argue and prepared to travel to the other side of the world, whilst my wife who, like me, was no more than a kid prepared to have our child. I was very unhappy.

There was still an atmosphere over the Blackpool drinking incident. The lads were aggrieved that the affair had been made so public. Barry Bridges told me they were particularly upset about getting off the train in London after being sent home and finding a welcome party of press and photographers. 'How did they know what train we were coming on, or if we were coming at all?' asked Barry. Doc and others at the club were still furious that the players would be so reckless as to go out on a session before such an important game and possibly jeopardise Chelsea's Championship chances. Of course, the players did not see it like that. They were young and young people can shrug off drinking copious amounts of alcohol with ease. Now if kick-off was at 9 a.m. on a Saturday after a Friday night bevy, it might have been different. More importantly, the incident had polarised the two main men at the club – Docherty and Venables.

Terry Venables was, still is, a character. Larger than life, he had a sharp brain, a quick wit and a charisma that attracted people to him. He was also a great captain. Venners, Allan Harris, Bert Murray, Bobby Tambling and Peter Bonetti had all joined the club on the same day as kids in 1958 and Terry had emerged as the ringleader of the younger element at the club. When Terry suggested something we all went along with it; when Terry cracked a joke we all laughed. Terry led and most people followed. The problem was that Docherty was the boss, not Terry, and it soon became obvious that the club was not big enough for the both of them. It was clear the manager was determined that there would be no breaches of discipline on the Australia trip. But six weeks in the sun, in the lager capital of the world, without drink for this Chelsea team was pushing it.

In a hotel in Melbourne, George Graham decided he was going to escape and asked who was joining him. About eight of us did and followed him over the wall, or at least through corridors and fire escapes, into the still, warm night air and to a bar where a party was being held that George strangely seemed to have some knowledge of. He was smooth on the pitch and he was smooth off it, was George. 'Gorgeous George' he was called then, and he could pull a bird faster than any man I had ever seen. Tommy Docherty liked winning, Terry Venables liked being liked and George Graham liked women.

Fortunately for everyone we got away with that late drink. Who knows, maybe Tommy Doc and Harry Medhurst were legless in the next bar down the street. A few days later in the hotel lounge Venables poked his head around the door and shouted 'Telegram at reception for you, Os.'

Remember telegrams? I think they became extinct about the same time as night watchmen with waste-bin fires and long torches. It was from Rose telling me that I was the father of a baby boy – Anthony John Osgood. It was 5 May 1965, and Tommy Docherty shook my hand warmly and told us we could all go out on the piss with his blessing.

Somewhere in Australia we were invited to visit a vineyard. I was offered a glass of wine by the hosts but looked over apprehensively at the Doc, who appeared to me to be draining a large glass of red. 'Can I?'

'Aye, son, absolutely. You're here to enjoy yourself. To work, rest and play and all that. Just relax,' and he accepted the glass that was originally offered to me.

Wine was a new experience for me and I knocked back three or four glasses in quick succession. I caught the eye of Joe Mears, our chairman, who seemed to be watching me. Joe leant over and whispered something in Tommy's ear. The Boss practically leapt over and smacked me round the head. 'What do you think you're playing at? Drinking! A lad of 17 as well!' and with a great sense of drama he took the glass from my hand and placed it firmly back on the table.

The Australia trip was a great success. We played an incredible 11 games in 6 weeks and took all the matches very seriously, winning all but 2 of them. It set us up well for the season and helped us gel altogether as a team. Tommy seemed to enjoy it and I felt that the Blackpool incident was now receding in importance for him and the players. The ice, I hoped, was beginning to thaw. My abiding memory of that tour is of airports as we hopped around from one part of Australia to another, leaving a sobbing girl in each place as George Graham said his goodbyes. Little did I know then that there would be another Blackpool incident quite soon, and this time involving me and only me.

Back in England the omens were good. I had played well in Australia and had worn the number nine shirt that Barry Bridges, our England international centre-forward, had made his own. For the first part of the tour Barry had been on England duty so I deputised, but when he joined up with us halfway through, instead of me dropping out for him, Barry was put out on the wing and I continued as number nine. Even though the opposition might not have been the toughest, my record of scoring 13 goals in 12 matches did encourage a few more people at the club to sit up and take notice. Just before the 1965–66 season kicked off Tom had a press day down at the Mitcham training ground we were now using. He was expert at keeping on the right side of the media, this day plying them with champagne and nibbles. 'I'd bet any one of you chaps that my young centre-forward Osgood could, if he tried a little harder, play for England. Not in the 1970 World Cup, but here in England next year,' I heard him claim.

Thanks Tom, but how about playing me in the first 11 first of all? I pulled him up a couple of weeks later, as I was not playing in the immediate pre-season matches, and again I asked to go on the transfer list. Tom was now getting fed up with my immature petulance and frustrated with my inability to see the bigger picture. A few months for me seemed like an age, for Tom it was nothing in the bigger scheme of things.

'Okay Peter,' he smiled (no Ossie now), 'I'll put the name P. Osgood on the circularised list to clubs and you know what?'

'What, boss?'

'They'll look at it and they'll think – who is P. Osgood? Paul, Philip, Patrick? Peter, you're a reserve team player. No one besides your mum, dad, brother and dog knows you.'

I was not in the first team when the season opened and the lads made a reasonable start. Bobby Tambling and Marvin Hinton picked up some injuries so when in September we were due to play Roma, the crack Italian side in the first round of the Fairs Cup, Doc told me I was in. He and Terry Venables must have been getting on better because they had been out to Italy together to watch the opposition and plan how we should deal with them. I, for one, was totally unprepared for their style of play, which was based on intimidation and openly kicking us. I didn't understand why, as they had such talent and skill – their centre-half, who was six inches smaller than me, beat me in the air every time and Barison, their winger, was playing magically. One of their players decided to spit in Eddie McCreadie's face and then seemed shocked when Eddie clean knocked him out and got himself sent off for retaliating. Terry Venables scored a hat trick and was on top form but the Italians didn't like it and also put him out of the game for a long period. George Graham got the fourth in our well-deserved 4–1 victory. In the second leg I was not picked and had no complaints.

We managed a goal-less draw and qualification for the next round, but by all accounts it was like a war zone out there, both on and off the pitch. That was the first time I realised that I was playing in a different league, literally, from Spital or even Chelsea reserves. When the stakes are high some players are prepared to injure one another. Before long I would experience a serious injury myself.

Docherty told me he thought I didn't try hard enough. Where had I heard that before? It was a refrain that had been with me all my life, and it would stay with me for the rest of it. Even Dad, my biggest fan, tried to gee me up and get me to run around the park more. Everyone, it seemed, wanted me to break into a sweat but my style of play had got me this far and what didn't come natural didn't seem right to me. The manager said I was sluggish in training and ordered me back in the afternoons when the other lads had returned to their wives, bars or golf courses for extra running, weight work and the dreaded 'doggies'. This meant running two legs of a forty-yard distance with no rest in between. I had to do three runs, six legs that is, all inside a fixed time. As you hit one time they reset it and gave you a smaller time limit. Besides being exhausting, I thought the exercise pretty stupid and had seen some of the chaps throw up their breakfasts during it. Nevertheless, it seemed to satisfy Tommy that I had learnt something, because he gave me my league debut at last.

The season was rolling on and the team was not living up to the promise of the previous campaign. Our home form in particular left a lot to be desired. I played my first league match at the Bridge against Newcastle and did little to impress in a boring and frustrating 1–1 draw. When I was straight back in the reserves the following week I couldn't moan. I was so tense and worried about making a mistake that I did not play my natural game. As soon as I got the ball I released it immediately, feeling that I should give it to someone better and more capable than I. Later Docherty pulled me over in training and said the best thing I could have wished for. 'Peter, I am playing you against Leicester in place of Barry Bridges. I guarantee you ten consecutive first team outings and I hope that takes the pressure off.'

It did. I was in the first team. I didn't have to worry whether I would be back in the reserves the following week, and I had time to build a rapport with my team mates. Tommy told me a few home truths that day too. He said I had to learn to be more ruthless, to work harder and to apply myself. I think teachers used to write stuff like this on my school report. Tommy summed it up by saying that I must stop regarding football as a game. That one really confused me, but I was not about to argue.

We lost 2–0 to Leicester but I played a little better than I had against Newcastle. I was very conscious about Barry Bridges sitting there on the substitutes' bench. He must have been gutted, knowing that being dropped couldn't be very healthy for his England international status. I would have been seething if I were him, being dropped for a kid that wasn't even playing that well. But Barry was a gentleman and was never nasty or bitter towards me. The crowd were though. You could not help but hear it; the chanting of Barry's name and cries to 'take the boy off and bring Barry on'. I suppose Tommy, shrewd man that he was, had foreseen this and that was why he gave me the guarantee of a run come what may. When Eddie Mac went off with an injury towards the end of the Leicester game and Barry trotted on, the place erupted.

I don't know what Tom had told Barry, but he put in a transfer request that unleashed a barrage of protests from the fans. I discovered later that Chelsea's number one supporter even then was a local chap called Mick Greenaway, and he was particularly attached to Barry. It was he, by all accounts, that had moved the more vociferous fans from the halfway line to the Shed End, as he rightly figured that the tin roof would provide amplification for their singing and chanting. Mick had been impressed by televised images of the 1962 World Cup, with fans singing and clapping in unison, and more recently had noticed the tangible effect Liverpool's musical Kop end seemed to be having on their team. Hard to believe as it is, literally just a few seasons before I joined, the home teams were still chivalrously clapping the opposition when they scored and at smaller grounds fans would swap ends at half-time so they could be behind the goal where hopefully their team would score. Mick organised a campaign that included a protest march when we played Sheffield United up there. The Chelsea fans hijacked a student march (of which there were plenty in that period) and unfurled banners saying 'Bridges must stay'. By bustling in at the front Greenaway had cheekily given the impression that he and his 40 or 50 pals were several hundred strong. What the university students made of the man that made the 'Zigger Zagger' chant famous is unknown. Following letters and calls to him and his wife, Barry withdrew his transfer request for the time being.

My fellow reserve and pal Jim McCalliog had also had enough

about this time. He asked for a transfer and Doc gave it to him. Sheffield Wednesday snapped him up and I was delighted for him at the end of the season when they reached the FA Cup final – Jim scored two goals for Wednesday in an entertaining and action-packed match that they eventually lost to Everton 3–2.

In the November I scored a blinding goal up at Villa Park that sealed a 4–2 win for us. There was a light snow and when the ball came to my feet not far past the halfway line I began to run forward with no real purpose in mind. I beat two Villa defenders, dummied another and before I knew it, it was just me and the goalie and I smashed past him with such force that the ball hit the net and rocketed straight out again and back into play. It was important because it was a good goal, so it built my profile in the papers and also my confidence.

I think I really won the Chelsea fans over in the New Year when we entertained Spurs at the Bridge. Spurs were yet to become Chelsea's bitterest rivals, as they are today, but they were a side everyone wanted to beat. Their early '60s Double triumph was still very fresh, although that side had largely broken up by then. Big Pat Jennings kept goal and Dave Mackay, a fearsome-looking Scot who would have looked more at home in a fairground boxing booth than on the football pitch, captained the team with a rod of iron. Dave was one of the most respected men in football. He was a hard man, but unlike some of his contemporaries did not go in for hurting people for the sake of it. He had broken his leg twice so he was only too aware of the damage that could be done. Jimmy Greaves and Alan Gilzean up front formed one of the best goal-poaching partnerships in the league. Nearly fifty thousand were crammed in and witnessed me lay on an equaliser for George Graham and then score the winner with a 25-yard shot that rocketed in to the top corner of the net, leaving Big Pat rooted to his line.

A couple of weeks later I scored a goal at Burnley's Turf Moor ground that many people regard as my best ever. Certainly, people refer to it even now, which is remarkable considering it happened nearly 40 years ago, and as far as I know no longer exists on film. I picked up the ball in my own half, beat Merrington, Talbot and John Angus, the Burnley defenders, and outpaced some others before driving it past Adam Blacklaw, the goalkeeper, as he came out to block me off. It felt good and I knew it was a creditable individual effort, but was taken aback over how excited everyone became. It must have looked better for the spectators than it felt for me.

As if to underline that this time I really had arrived I was called up for the England Under-23 side to play Scotland Under-23s in a fixture at Roker Park, then Sunderland's ground. Tommy Hughes, the reserve keeper to Peter Bonetti at Chelsea, was playing for Scotland. It was bitterly cold and snowing. Alf Ramsey, as he was then, spoke to us all in the dressing-room. I was fascinated by his voice; he had a sort of strangulated public schoolboy accent, spoken through practically closed lips as if he were training to be a ventriloquist. He was, though, a working-class boy like almost all footballers, so I can only imagine he worked on his voice because for some reason he felt that as England manager he needed to project a certain image. I told him that I had a nagging injury and wasn't sure I'd be able to last the full 90 minutes. 'Score a goal, son, and I'll bring you straight off. How's that?' he smiled.

I obliged and Alf was as good as his word and brought me off. Mind you, the rest of the teams came off ten minutes later as the game was abandoned due to the snow, and my international goal slipped through the record books and history.

Our season was getting better as we progressed in the League, the Fairs Cup and the FA Cup. I was scoring goals and getting lots of press coverage. Predictions were being made about an England future for me and Tommy himself was praising me up to the eyeballs to all and sundry. Suddenly I was getting fan mail, autograph hunters queued to catch me before and after games and training. People I had never met were inviting me to parties and functions. Press photographers would call over to me as I parked my car on arrival at the ground and I would be thrilled later to see the picture in the paper or one of the football magazines. After a while it would have worried me if the press boys weren't taking my picture. Back in Windsor people pointed at me in the street. In Dedworth nothing had changed, but me and Rose both realised I was now a celebrity, a famous person, a VIP – whatever they called it – and all sorts of people wanted a piece of me. I loved it. Who doesn't love being the centre of attention? Especially at 19 years of age, when fame seems like the ultimate gift that could be bestowed on you.

Almost as quickly as the celebrity status came the money. With win bonuses, European appearances and suchlike I was earning up to £200 a week. To put that into perspective, the average wage around 1966–67 would have been around £20 per week, and I was pulling in around 10 times that much. That would be the equivalent of about

£200,000 to £250,000 a year in today's money. Imagine that – close on five grand a week at 19! It would be pretty rich (excuse the pun) for me to complain about our lot compared to that of today's footballers, some of whom are earning 30 grand a week and more. We were bloody well paid, especially compared to the ordinary working man, which is what we would have been if not lucky enough to make it in football (and many would become again after their careers were over), and wealthy beyond our wildest dreams.

My only issue is that as very young men we were given too much money. We had no real guidance on how to invest, how to save and how to spend, but most of us would have taken no notice anyway. As footballers we reach our lifetime's earning peak at a time when we don't think we have a lifetime. Like all other young people we were living for the moment and were reckless with our love, our money and our futures. People who knew much better than us kids should have compulsorily invested half our wages in a sort of pension/savings scheme that we couldn't touch until the age of 35 unless our careers finished prematurely. I'm sure I could have scraped by on the equivalent of two and a half grand a week, and by the time I retired from the game I would have been looking at a fund that, with rolled-up interest, could have been worth between two and three million in today's money.

We didn't finish the season too badly at fifth in the League, but Barcelona dumped us out the Fairs Cup and after an exciting FA Cup run where we disposed of Leeds and Liverpool we succumbed to a not-so-hot Sheffield Wednesday side in the semi-final. They beat us 2–0 in a hard match in poor conditions at Villa Park. They were such a large side! Big Northern men like Vic Mobley, Wilf Smith and Gerry Young were hard to beat and you half expected them to have a whippet or two running alongside them. With the exception of a couple of players there was not an ounce of flair between them, but that day they effectively prevented us from playing.

To Tommy Docherty this was an abject failure. Personally I thought it was not a bad season, but he set about publicly breaking the team up. He had already taken the captaincy away from Terry Venables and given it to Ron Harris, a move that didn't go down too well with Venners. Apparently some other players had been offered the job but refused, and this show of solidarity wound Tom up even more. He transfer-listed Terry along with George Graham and Barry Bridges. Ken Shellito's career had sadly reached the end of the road due to injury and Peter Bonetti had also asked for a transfer. Terry went to Spurs,

George to Arsenal and Barry to Birmingham. Peter Bonetti stayed, even though Tom had brought Alex Stepney in from Millwall to replace him, and Tommy Baldwin came from Arsenal as part exchange for George. One day Docherty popped up to Dundee and returned with a quiet little man named Charlie Cooke. So whilst one great team was disintegrating, the pieces of the next were being put into place.

My league debut season had been satisfactory. I managed 11 league and cup goals in 47 total appearances – better than the two goals and one League Cup appearance of the previous season. More importantly, I had played competitive football now against the biggest names in the game: Gordon Banks, Derek Dougan, Billy Bremner, Jackie Charlton, Johnny Giles, Bobby Moore, Geoff Hurst, Martin Peters, Tommy Smith, Ian St John, Pat Jennings, Dave Mackay, Jimmy Armfield, Bobby Robson (am I that old?), Ray Wilson, Jim Baxter, Denis Law, Bobby Charlton and George Best. It's easy to forget the buzz of playing against these stars for the first time, but when you're a green teenager, fresh off the building site, jumping for a ball shoulder to shoulder with Bobby Charlton, for example, it is quite surreal.

If that close season was turbulent at Chelsea, it was tumultuous in the country as a whole. England won the World Cup at Wembley in the historic 4–2 victory over West Germany. I had been flabbergasted to have been named in Alf's selected 40 players for the tournament, but not surprised and therefore not too disappointed not to make the final squad of 22. Ironically Chelsea were on a pre-season tour in Germany when the most famous English football match ever took place, and we watched it on a small television in a bar with a bunch of friendly locals. It was a fantastic achievement. Alf fashioned that team into exactly what he visualised from the day he took the job as England manager and winning the World Cup was the ultimate example of planning, practice and execution. Alf, never a man motivated by money, should have retired as England manager then. His hero status could never have been touched and maybe the ultimate powers in football would have had little choice but to elevate him to a place among them, and he could have influenced the overall management of football. As it was he soldiered on when the only way was down and left himself vulnerable to far lesser beings than himself. I really do remember thinking as I watched him exercising amazing self-restraint during the celebrations after the game, 'Enjoy it Alf, because it doesn't get any better than this.'

Nearly 20 years later, but strangely again at Wembley, I had the same feeling when Bob Geldof stood up and acknowledged the crowd in the stadium (and in every corner of the planet) at the Live Aid concert he had organised. I know his motives were entirely charitable, but I felt slightly sad for him knowing that the rest of his life was going to be lived in the shadow of those few moments. On a smaller scale, by 1985, I was talking from experience.

The euphoria of winning the World Cup continued well into the next season, 1966–67. It must have been the most keenly anticipated English football season ever; each of the 11 World Cup-winning players were national heroes and household names, and Alf Ramsey was revered on a par with Winston Churchill. The opportunity to watch them all back in domestic action was something even previous non-football fans did not want to miss. Gates were up and morale was high – in football and in the country. Harold Wilson was Prime Minister and he had famously awarded OBEs to The Beatles, who had become the biggest thing, not only in England, but also in America. For the Yanks to be idolising four lads from Liverpool rather than us salivating over celluloid icons such as Marilyn Monroe, Elvis Presley or Cary Grant was yet another boost to the country's burgeoning self-esteem.

Mods and Rockers fought very public battles on our beaches among the sandcastles, stripy deckchairs and snoring men with handkerchiefs tied on their heads – old and new England colliding. The Mods loved their clothes and the girls especially would parade up and down the Kings Road, just as the Punk Rockers would a decade later. Mini-skirts and kinky boots were on mass display, as every girl wanted to become a Lulu, a Twiggy or an Emma Peel. It was a sizzling time to be alive and young, and it was beyond description to be a famous footballer whose stamping ground was the Kings Road, Chelsea.

Our campaign got off to a flying start and ten games in we beat an upcoming Manchester City side 4–1 at Maine Road to sit on top of the League. I netted one and Bobby Tambling, Tommy Baldwin and Joe Kirkup, a good full-back from West Ham, the other three between them. I should have been flattered, but at the end of this game the City fans started chanting 'Osgood, No Good' to the tune of the chimes of Big Ben. Stupidly, because I wasn't really ruffled, I raised two fingers to them and got reported to the Football Association. The acrimony of the close season, sparked by the Doc's ruthless shuffling of the team, soon dissolved in the excitement of our opening form. We were a happy ship when we headed up on the train on the night of 5 October 1966 for a League Cup third-round tie with Second Division Blackpool. Chelsea were a real family club then, with the directors, players and supporters often travelling away on the same train.

It was a foggy night, and when the match kicked off most of the population of the United Kingdom were safely indoors, in front of their black-and-white televisions watching *Coronation Street*. They would have been sympathising with poor old Minnie Caldwell, devastated that her lodger, the cheeky young tearaway Jed Stone, had just been carted off to prison. Nevertheless 13,520 souls were prepared to miss the soap (no videos then, remember) and make their way to Bloomfield Road. Ron Sturt, who would later join Tommy at Chelsea, managed Blackpool at that time.

The match went to form as Peter Houseman, who was also breaking into the first team, took a pass from me and sliced a ball through Blackpool's defence and into the net. Their confident young defender Emlyn Hughes was on my case right from the start and after he tackled me from behind I was determined to give him a kick back just to show him I was no pushover. The chance came as we both raced towards a 50/50 ball. Our legs crunched. I heard it, Emlyn heard it and the crowd heard it as the bone above my ankle snapped. The crowd had fallen silent in anticipation of the tackle and as my leg splintered the sickening noise seemed to reverberate around the ground. I imagined everyone closing their eyes and wincing as one. Putting my hand down to my leg I could feel the bone through my sock and I waved weakly for help. Emlyn picked himself up and walked away without a glance behind him. Our players shouted and swore at him but he didn't respond.

Norman Medhurst, son of trainer Harry, was with us that day and he knelt down beside me and cradled my left leg.

'Does it hurt Ossie?'

'No Norman, you've got the wrong leg.'

When he gently rolled down the sock on my right leg and saw the bone protruding he went white and seemed to rock backward and forward. I thought we would need two stretchers, one for me and one for him. They got me on the stretcher and as I disappeared down the tunnel I caught the eye of a supporter. His face was contorted with hate, his lips curled and his eyes bulged as he spat, 'Serves you fucking right, Osgood.'

That upset me temporarily more than breaking my leg. What had I done to warrant such hate? This was a game of football, wasn't it? But then I remembered Tommy Docherty's words, 'This is not a game, son.' Now I knew what he meant.

Tommy came into the changing-room as we waited for the ambulance. Our eyes met and I must have looked to him like a child searching for comfort from a parent. For the first time I welled up. 'This is it, isn't it Boss? I'm finished, aren't I?'

Tommy was upset too and this alarmed me at first, but he fixed his eyes on me and said firmly, 'Son, mark my words, you'll come back from this a better player.'

He said it with such conviction that I believed him and it lifted me.

Dr Boyne, the Chelsea doctor, took one look at the leg and called an ambulance, and off we went to Blackpool's Victoria hospital. It was there that Dr Boyne made a decision that may well have saved my career. When we got to the casualty department a duty doctor took a rudimentary look at me and said, 'Yep, we'll get that set.'

Dr Boyne was not happy and asked if a surgeon was available but was told none were on duty. 'We'll wait until one is then,' he insisted. And I'm glad he had that presence of mind, for I was in no fit state to get picky. Many a player has not come back from a broken leg due to badly set breaks. I was operated on that night, put in plaster, dosed up with painkillers and fit enough to join the players and officials on the train journey back to London in the morning. Throughout the ordeal I had not removed my Chelsea shirt.

On the journey home the lads told me about an incident that had happened the previous night while I was in the hospital. Alan Skirton, a Blackpool player who had been at Arsenal, had arranged a party and a few of the lads had decided to go along. Alan was nicknamed Fish because he was said to drink like one. Stan Flashman, a larger-than-life character, was with our party. Stan was a big chap and the country's number one ticket tout. He could get you a ticket for anywhere: Wembley, Wimbledon, Madison Square Garden – you name it. He popped up all over the place and made friends with many players. I suppose he had to as we (players that is) were the source of many of his tickets. On the other hand we were also good customers. Stan was like a cross between Arthur Daley and Frank Cannon the American TV detective, and it helped his reputation that he was rumoured to know a few of the underworld faces.

Tommy Hughes was our reserve team goalkeeper by this time and some said he bore more than a passing physical resemblance to myself. Tommy came out of the toilet and Emlyn Hughes spotted him. 'Looks like Osgood made a quick recovery,' he wisecracked. None of our lot saw the funny side and Stan Flashman lunged his large frame at Hughes. His team mates stood between them and made sure Emlyn was packed off home before things turned nasty. I bear no grudge against Emlyn Hughes. After all, my leg got better – he's still got that silly fucking voice.

Ossie was one of the most gifted players I ever played with or against. He was reliable too, always last in the cross-country runs along with Marvin Hinton and John Dempsey. A goal he scored against Burnley where he wasted almost their whole side before beating Blacklaw, the keeper, was without doubt the finest I have ever seen. Some point to his poor disciplinary record, but he had to look after himself out there because he was the one the others wanted to bring down. One hot day he said to us all in the changing-rooms, 'Don't you lot start hitting long balls for me to chase because I ain't running in this weather.' He was serious. That was Ossie for you.

R. Harris, Businessman

5

What's Up Doc?

WHEN THE ADRENALIN HAD SUBSIDED A DAY OR SO AFTER THE BREAK, THE reality of the situation hit me. I would be out of the team for three months minimum – just when I had established a regular first team place, emerged as Chelsea's main goalscorer and was knocking on the door of the England team. Would I ever be as good again? Plenty of players were never the same after a leg break. Would I get back in the first team? If they developed a rapport without me I might struggle. These thoughts and others tortured me in those early weeks in plaster. Not only was my playing career brought to a halt but so was my lifestyle. By now I was beginning to get into tune with what people wanted me to be and starting to accept invitations for a piss-up here and a party there. I had just stepped onto the roller-coaster only to stumble and fall off.

Unfortunately poor Rose took the brunt of my frustration at being housebound and my corrosive fretting over my career. She did everything for me at that time and it must have been just like having another baby to care for. Except this one effed and blinded all day long rather than gurgled and cried. The club were marvellous though, and did everything they could to put me at ease and make me feel a part of things still. I am forever grateful to Tommy Docherty and the Chelsea board for helping us buy our first house in Testwood Road, Windsor, courtesy of an interest-free loan. Stan Quantrell would often come in the club minibus and take me to Mitcham to watch the training and eventually do a bit of physio with Harry Medhurst, or to the ground to join in whatever was going on there.

When Tommy signed Tony Hateley from Aston Villa, though, it sent me plummeting back into a state of paranoia. Tony was a big centre-forward who was banging the goals in like a machine up at Villa Park and was tipped as the next England number nine. He was particularly lethal with his head. His forehead was unusually large and a good cross would find it hard to miss; sections of the crowd compared him to Herman Munster, the Frankenstein-like character with a bolt through his neck played by Fred Gwynne on the TV at the time. We got on fine, Tony and me, and he and his wife stayed with Rose and me at Windsor for a while. I'd be lying, though, if I didn't admit that I was relieved when he didn't seem to hit it off at Chelsea. He never really put together a run of form and the fickle Chelsea crowd did not take him to their hearts. It was rumoured that Tommy Doc was regretting this £100,000 signing, a club record at the time, but he would have been very reluctant to admit it. Tommy must have thought all his prayers had been answered when the phone rang and the inimitable growl of Bill Shankly, boss of Liverpool, could be heard at the other end of the line.

'Tommy. The boy Hateley. I hear he's a wee bit unsettled.'

The Doc could not resist moving straight into negotiating mode. 'Bill, I have to tell you now – 100,000 wouldn't buy him.'

'Aye, and I'm fucking one of them,' retorted Shanks, never one to be taken for a mug, before slamming the phone down.

Insecurity ate away inside of me. At one point I called a national newspaper and told them that I thought I could never fit into the Chelsea side again. What did I expect? Dozens of telephone calls from First Division managers saying 'Never fear Ossie, there is always a place for you in our team'? The only manager that called was Tommy Doc himself, demanding to know what I was playing at. 'Why are you saying things like that to the papers?'

He seemed really injured that I had done so. He reminded me that Chelsea were still paying my wages, sending me tickets for games and looking after me generally. Of course, he was right, but I was like a stroppy teenager craving reassurance.

Tony Hateley did eventually move to Liverpool and carried on moving, passing through Notts County and Coventry City among others. Every time they paid £100,000 or so and I don't think he asked to go on the list any of the times, so I think and hope he clocked up plenty of transfer fee percentages. Younger readers will know that his son Mark surpassed even his father's achievements, playing regularly for England in the 1980s.

Rose was relieved when I started getting out of the house again. Bill Knight, a lovely old boy from Windsor, and a digger driver by profession, took to coming and picking me up and taking me out rabbiting with his ferret in the local woods, or we'd go further afield to places like Dorset and Teignmouth and do some sea-fishing. Other pals drove me around and we filled empty days by visiting country pubs. I was drinking more, as I had more time, and because I was not able to work it off, the alcohol soon translated into pounds – 28 to be exact. Still I was hopeful that I would be fit in time for the FA Cup final that Chelsea had reached without me and with no little help from a brilliant Tony Hateley goal against Leeds in the semi-final – a match I had watched from the dugout with Tommy Doc. Tottenham Hotspur were to be the opponents and Terry Venables, our old team mate and captain, had already made his mark there.

One trip out, though, was almost a disaster. I now had the time and money to take up golf and I took to it well. It is the first-choice leisure activity of footballers, fitting in well with their working patterns and their relative affluence. My uncle, Bob Snashall, had ferried me to a nine-hole course at Datchet, and during the course of the game my leg plaster split open and I did something dodgy to my break. The doctor told me that I had been bloody stupid walking around a golf course on my leg and had delayed my recovery by some weeks. The bad news was I definitely would not be fit for the 1967 FA Cup final and the good news was that I would still make a recovery and play again – eventually.

The night before the final we stayed at the Kensington Palace Hotel and in the morning travelled by coach to Wembley. The lads were not at all nervous and some sang along to 'Puppet on a String', the song that Sandie Shaw had won the Eurovision Song Contest with a few Saturdays previously. I was not in the mood, however much front I put on. If you're not playing you're not part of it, it's as simple as that. You can walk out with the team, inspect the turf in your suit and tie and get on the pitch at the end to join in the celebrations, but essentially you are an interloper, not even a bit-part player in the history that is being made around you.

Spurs were the better side on the afternoon, Jimmy Robertson putting them ahead just before half-time and Frank Saul adding to the lead in the second half. Bobby Tambling pulled one back for us near the end of the game but we never really looked like winning. Losing a cup final is worse than not making the final at all, and we left Wembley with our tails between our legs. Doc and the players were obviously crushed but on reflection it was not as bad a season as he imagined – ninth in the League and FA Cup finalists. As far as I was concerned there was still a momentum at the club. I felt that I had not even got into my stride yet and the likes of Charlie Cooke, Eddie McCreadie, John Hollins and Tommy Baldwin were just as good as any of the players that had moved on.

Ron Suart, the assistant manager, personally presided over the campaign to get me fit for the 1967–68 season. He was particularly worried about the limp I had developed and the weight I had stuck on. Now was not a time when I could afford to be lazy and he worked me and worked me, knowing I would not work myself unattended. He was like Burgess Meredith, the trainer in the *Rocky* films, bollocking and cajoling me and we had the whole training ground more or less to ourselves. The other bastards were in America on a pre-season tour and I was jealous and bitter about not being with them, but with hindsight it was a good thing for me. Without other distractions Ron and I got down to business and as each week went by I could feel the leg becoming less stiff and the aches and pains disappearing. By the time the season started and I had played in a couple of friendlies, Ron and I both told the Doc I was fit to play.

But I wasn't really – or I had lost my confidence. The first match of the season was up at the Hawthorns against West Bromwich Albion and although we snatched a victory, my performance was dire. For the next few matches the manager persevered with me, but I was useless and everyone knew it. Tommy told me not to worry and assured me the form would come, but he would say that wouldn't he? A deep depression began to envelop me and I began to think in terms of my little career before my broken leg as being it. I'd have to ply my trade in the lower divisions and leagues or retire from the game completely. I could hear in my mind supporters chatting below the Bovril Bar at Stamford Bridge in years to come:

'Remember that kid Osgood, he was looking good for a while. What happened to him?'

'Broke a leg, didn't he? Never the same after.'

It got worse. Newcastle, who had only just escaped relegation last season, walloped us 5–1 and then Southampton, another club who tended to look up the First Division at all the others, walloped us 6–2 at Stamford Bridge. Ron Davies, the Welsh centre-forward, fired four and a lad called Martin Chivers scored the other two. The only small consolation was that I broke my duck and scored – both our goals in fact – and played much better than I had been. My first goal was one of my best up until then as I swayed past five Southampton players before finding the net. I heard later that Terry Paine, the former England player and Southampton's greatest servant, was going to bring me down by whipping my legs from beneath me but decided they were 3–0 up and therefore not desperate, and he did not want to risk damaging my recovering leg.

The Doc brought me down, though, afterwards by telling me I still had a long way to go and not to get excited about one game. It was after that match. I noticed him under pressure for the first time. The press wanted to know what was going wrong and Tommy tried to laugh it off by saying it was just one of those things. One thing the press won't take is complacency or flippancy when the going gets tough. They demand naked contrition. If Tom had bared his soul and agonised over Chelsea's predicament they probably wouldn't have gone for the jugular, but he didn't seem to give a shit what they thought. As we threaded our way through the press men and photographers out on the forecourt he put his hand on my shoulder and said almost distantly, 'Ossie, who knows where our futures will take us.' I thought that rather strange.

We managed to overcome Sheffield United at the Bridge next but lost to Liverpool at Anfield, and it didn't help the team or me that my nemesis, Tony Hateley, scored twice. By now we were floundering near the bottom of the table, the life was draining out of us. I scored in a draw with Stoke City next but we went down 3–0 the next Saturday to Nottingham Forest. One of their goals was scored by Ian Storey-Moore, who at the time was the only other footballer in Division One that had three Os in his surname besides me. That was interesting, wasn't it?

A boring home draw against Coventry City the following Saturday was Tommy's last in charge of Chelsea Football Club. We suspected something was amiss on the Friday when Tommy was called into the office after training had finished. The press were hanging around the forecourt next to the Shed End and so were we. The Doc appeared at the boardroom door, muttered something and then closed it. Just like in a scene from a Hollywood thriller, the press boys turned on the balls of their feet and ran for the phone boxes outside the ground. We knew then that was it. Us players didn't know how to react. Most of us had fallen out with the man at some time or another but we liked and admired him. You always knew where you stood with Tommy Docherty. He'd been good to me: signed me, gave me my break, stuck with me now when I clearly was not the same player as before my leg snapped, helped me buy a house, bought me drinks, told me jokes. And really, whose fault was it we were not playing well? Not Tommy Doc's. We'd already proved that this team had ability and talent – the fact we weren't turning it on was down to us, not Tommy. And that's why some of us hung around the car park awkwardly – guilt. His wife Agnes pulled into the car park in their Jaguar and Tommy came out of the door and hopped in. Before they pulled away he rolled down the passenger window and held out his hand. Ron Harris, our skipper, shook it. 'All the best Ron,' he smiled.

None of us really knew what to say and, self-conscious about the press and snappers around us, allowed him to speed out of Stamford Bridge for the last time. Marvin Hinton and myself felt we hadn't said our goodbyes or expressed how we felt about him leaving and we went to his house a couple of days later. He tried to put a brave face on it but was not his usual ebullient self, and I could tell he was gutted although he was not a man to show emotion, other than anger.

Tom thinks his days were numbered when Joe Mears, the chairman, died. He and Joe got on well and Joe believed in letting the manager manage, but his successor Bill Pratt tended to interfere. There was some sort of spat between them after Tommy was suspended for some remarks he made to an official on the Barbados pre-season tour. Mr Pratt wanted to know how Tommy could expect to manage the side when he was suspended. Pratt by name, pratt by nature, was Tom's feeling on the matter and he told the man to his face that he would find it hard to work with someone who knew absolutely nothing about football.

Tommy has become a good friend. We reminisce and laugh about those days when we meet. He's a nice man, and one of the few people I can honestly say have really influenced my life. His contribution to the game has not been fully appreciated. It is generally accepted that outspoken managers who said what they thought didn't come along until Brian Clough, but the Doc was at it six or seven years earlier. Like Clough, he could motivate previously average players into exceptional ones – surely the sign of a great manager.

People sometimes ask me why I didn't become a manager when

my playing career ended. It might have something to do with the fact that no one ever asked me and that I never applied for a managerial post. I couldn't manage myself, let alone others. But even if I had been asked and I was cut out for the job, I wouldn't do it. There are only so many honours up for grabs each season and they are to be shared between 15 or so of the 90-odd league clubs. Nowadays it seems the remaining 75 are branded as failures, which is rubbish. The average tenure of a manager is now ridiculously short and no one is given enough time to build a team, let alone a culture and an organisation. How can anyone be judged and executed on the strength of a string of poor results, sometimes as few as three or four? Think of all the managers that were once flavour of the month and have now been almost entirely forgotten: John Bond, Gordon Lee, Gordon Jago and Ron Saunders to name a few off the top of my head. These men, who all achieved considerable success suddenly became useless, did they? It defies logic. If I were offered the opportunity to become a manager I would get a non-financial clause written into my contract while my bargaining power was high, i.e. when they had approached me. I would insist on a minimum contract for an entire season, whatever point in the year I joined, and a clause whereby I couldn't be sacked unless the team's performance was worse than the previous season. This would take into account position in the League, and progress in cups. It would ensure a decent crack of the whip, give some protection against short-term attitudes and help a manager ride the inevitable runs of poor form.

My personal trainer Ron Suart took the reins in a caretaker manager role, but the lads were devastated. We even spoke to each other about relegation and when we travelled up to Leeds the next day we shamefully and openly discussed how many goals we might lose by! Seven, it turned out. That Leeds team were dirty bastards, but they were good, and no one had the spirit to really get into them. On the score-sheet that day was one Albert Johanneson, who (along with John Charles at West Ham) was one of the only two black players in the First Division at the time. I saw a sad TV documentary a couple of years back where I learned that Albert had died living rough in Yorkshire as a down and out. This was our nadir. Chelsea were looking down and out.

Dave Sexton, our former coach, who was now with Arsenal following spells with Orient and Fulham, was tempted back to take over as manager and Ron Suart was nudged back to the wings. I already respected Dave, he was an excellent coach, a deep thinker and a grafter, but I wondered how he would fare as overall boss. I would soon find out.

Immediately he explained to us what his strategy was going to be. He said that it was too ambitious to change everything at once – he'd start with the defence and when that was shored up, concentrate on the midfield and then the forward line. He worked on tactics with Ron Harris, Eddie McCreadie and Marvin Hinton and almost immediately things stopped getting worse. We stopped getting hammered week in, week out at least. Then he went to work on the midfield and we started creating attacks again. By this time us boys up front were reaping the benefits. Confidence started coursing through our veins and towards the end of the season we were rocking, to such an extent that from being relegation candidates in November we finished the season in a highly respectable sixth place and reached the quarter-finals of the FA Cup. I played in all 42 league games and scored 16 goals in the end. On the whole this was achieved with the same pool of players that were performing so badly at the start of the season, so who knows if it would have happened anyway under Tommy? Dave signed Alan Birchenall, a striker from Sheffield United whose most distinctive feature was his blond hair; personally I thought he was a ringer for Mae West, only more feminine. He also signed Dave Webb from Southampton and later John Dempsey from Fulham.

Still, whether the team would have been more successful under Tommy or Dave was academic. Dave was in charge, there was no doubt about it; he knew what he wanted and we were left in no doubt that he would get it.

I started supporting the Blues in 1963 and religiously kept a scrapbook of cuttings dominated by the two Peters, Osgood and Bonetti, my two special favourites. I also had a picture of Ossie and Racquel Welch on my wall; only when I reached a certain age did I start to find Racquel more attractive than Ossie.

When I was on *This is Your Life* a few years back, the highlight of the evening (and perhaps my life) was the screen going back and there were Ossie, Hutch, Chopper and The Cat standing there. A moment to savour that brought tears to my eyes.

It has taken Chelsea 30 years to find a player of similar stature to Ossie and that is Gianfranco Zola. He shares the same silky skills and loyalty to the fans and club that Peter Osgood has. I think it is sad how Peter has been treated by Chelsea in recent times. He is a hero to thousands and we, the fans, like having him around.

C. Mantle, Actor

6

Dandies on the Kings Road

A TESTAMENT TO THE COACHING SKILLS OF DAVE SEXTON WAS THE STRANGE case of Ian Hutchinson. He paid £5,000 to non-league Cambridge for him and frankly when I first saw Hutch I thought it was about £4,995 too much. He was a tall, gangly boy with a disarming lop-sided grin, but precious little evidence of any footballing skills. He couldn't trap a bag of cement. In training he seemed clumsy and out of his depth, I was sure that Dave or whoever had spotted and recommended him had made a mistake. However, it could not be a big one as five grand was a piffling fee by now in the spiralling transfer market. Birch, for example, had set us back £100,000 and Leeds would soon set a new record by signing Leicester's Allan Clarke for £165,000. My sister Mandy was a better player than Hutch in those first days. Seriously, she was about 30 years ahead of her time was Amanda Osgood. She loved football and played it all the time as a kid, like I did. Had the women's game been as developed then as it is now, I'm sure she would have been the leading light. Dave must have seen something in Hutch though and he worked with him meticulously. Somehow he flowered and as I will tell became a key plank in this exciting and flourishing Chelsea team. He became a favourite with the fans, and his long throw became the stuff of legend. The throw was extraordinary, he seemed to be able to launch the ball from the halfway line deep into the opposition's penalty area, and it became a lethal asset in our ever-increasing box of tricks.

Tommy Baldwin, too, had become a firm favourite of the Shed End.

To the tune of 'MacNamara's Band' they greeted his arrival on the pitch with:

> His name is Tommy Baldwin,
> He's the leader of the team,
> What team?
> The finest football team that the world has ever seen,
> We're the Fulham Road supporters and we're louder than the
> Kop,
> If anyone wants to argue,
> We'll kill the f*****g lot.

Charming. Tommy was nicknamed Sponge, for what reason I'm not sure. Some said it was connected to his on-field style of play but I guessed it had more to do with his ability to soak up the drink. Tommy was a top scooper. He loved the ladies too and found himself at the centre of a tabloid scrum when he formed a relationship with Gabrielle Crawford, the wife of actor Michael Crawford, who was soon to be immortalised as the hapless Frank Spencer in the TV programme *Some Mothers Do 'Ave 'Em*. He was a leading British actor, having starred in hit films such as *The Knack* and *The Jokers*. The story goes that Michael tried in vain many times to persuade his wife to accompany him to Chelsea games but she had no interest in football. When she did finally relent, she met Sponge and the rest is history. Tommy and Gabrielle went on to have two children together.

The following little story wasn't Tommy, but the player in question was married at the time and still is. To the same wife. So when I tell it these days I use Tommy's name. Sorry mate. He'd pulled a bird on the town after the game and given her some sweet talk to smooth his wicked way. Tommy returned to London but was a bit concerned when the girl continued to contact him. The next time we played in this particular town a message was sent to Tommy via the hotel we were staying in. It was from the girl's brothers, who swore they were going to shoot him at today's game. Sponge took the threat very seriously and showed us the letter, hands shaking. Go and see the boss, we advised. A white-faced Tommy Baldwin went to see Tommy Docherty and recounted the whole sorry story. The Doc sat quietly throughout, apparently deep in thought.

Finally he said, 'When you get out on that pitch today, Tommy, just keep running. A moving target is much harder to hit.'

Dad, sister Amanda & Mum on a day out sometime in the late 1960s.

At home in Kentons Lane, Dedworth. Steve Bourne, Amanda, Cousin Ray, myself and Jenny, my lovely old dog.

Spital Old Boys. Brother Mick is at the end of the front row holding a trophy. I'm standing behind him. Les Marks in suit crouches at front.

Harry Medhurst laughs at my ball control
on the pitch at Stamford Bridge.

Rains stops play. The boys come in after training. From L-R: Ron Harris, John Boyle, me, Eddie McCreadie, Peter Houseman, Joe Kirkup, Bobby Tambling, Peter Bonetti and Jimmy Andrews.

Numbers 7, 8 and 9. Barry Bridges, George Graham and myself.

The Doc talks to Marvin Hinton, Ron Harris, Eddie McCreadie
and myself among others. I'm more interested in the camera,
even then.

Fan mail. As my
confidence grows, so do
my sideburns.

Mexico 1970. Nobby Stiles is saying
'Where's the bracelet?'

Even this didn't impress Sir Alf enough to play me against Brazil.

In the bath after winning the FA Cup in 1970. We're all on bubbly but Chopper's milk is on the ledge.

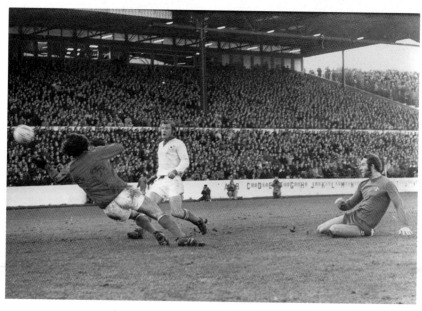

Scoring against Leicester City. Peter Shilton dives, Dennis Rofe looks on.

Holidays in the sun. Back row: Paddy Mulligan, Steve Kember, Tony Frewin, Ron Harris, Chris Garland. Front row: Harry Medhurst, Peter Bonetti, Peter Houseman and me.

'Blue is the Colour'. Top of the Pops 1972. From L-R: Billy Digweed, John Hollins, Micky Droy, Ron Harris, Marvin Hinton, Tommy Baldwin, Charlie Cooke, Me, Jimmy Savile (or is it Chris Garland?), John Dempsey, John Phillips and Eddie McCreadie.

Pop Idols. Huddy and me. He knew the words off by heart. I didn't.

Racquel Welch wearing the kit.
She was big at the time.

Tommy was a grafter on the field. He didn't have the silky dribbling skills of Charlie Cooke or the physical presence of myself and because of that his contribution to the team is sometimes underrated. It shouldn't be, because he was always there, getting busy up front, scoring goals and creating chances for me and others. He played in four finals, never forget, and was that vital cog that allowed us all to be what we were. When I was researching the meaning of my surname I stumbled across Baldwin – it is Old English for 'brave friend'. Very apt.

Our skipper Ron Harris would take a drink, but he was not one to over-indulge like Tommy, Eddie, Charlie and myself. Harris is a good old English name, conjuring up images of such heroes as Bomber, Anita and Keith of Orville fame. Ron was nicknamed Chopper. It had nothing to do with his anatomy, but was a reference to his uncompromising tackling style. (Actually we all called him Buller, because he did tend to lean towards bullshit in everyday conversation.) The three main hard men of the period were Norman 'Bite Yer Legs' Hunter up at Leeds, Tommy Smith at Liverpool and our own Chopper Harris. He was not a big man but I can honestly say that I'd prefer to face Hunter or Smith than Ron on the football field. I certainly avoided him in training. One time I saw him take Keith Weller out in a five-a-side match for having the audacity to refer to Ron's wife as a taxi. Ron couldn't drive, which was a godsend because he couldn't really see either, and Lee, his wife, would collect him from training in their Mini Clubman. Weller had only just joined us and should have known better than to wind Ron up. We all looked the other way as Keith writhed in agony, but Sexton went berserk. 'Ronnie! What are you doing you mad bastard?' Remember, Dave had just paid a lot of money for Weller. 'He should learn to keep his mouth shut,' shrugged Ron. Keith was out for a month.

Off the pitch he wouldn't say boo to a goose. It was a constant source of amusement to us all that he still called his parents 'mummy and daddy' and that he tended to dress in 'sensible' cardigans and slacks. Mind you, he's had the last laugh there – by not succumbing to the fat ties, flowery shirts and long collars of the period, when we look back over old photographs he's the only one that does not have to cringe. (I pity Alan Ball, who had to deal with the indignity of having some Mexico 1970 World Cup snaps resurrected in the papers recently where he was caught – bang to rights – wearing a cravat!) Ron was the only one of us at the time who was keeping an eye on his future and he invested in a sweet shop in Ewell, Surrey.

When I was living near him I used to pick him up in my car. For a while I was using a Ford Cortina 1600E loaned to me by the England set-up. You had the option to buy after a year, but as it was conspicuous with red and white stripes, I didn't really fancy it. When waiting for Ron I once dipped my hand into the lemon bon-bon jar and pulled out a few. As we flew up the A3 and I was sucking on the sweets, Ron said, 'I hope you're going to pay for those sweets, Os.' I still don't know whether he was joking or not.

We had our routines in training, such as four-mile runs, ball work and the much-loved five-a-side games often played in the forecourt at Stamford Bridge. Sometimes these games were played with more fervour and spirit than the real thing. Incredibly, word got around about the kickabouts and sometimes up to a couple of hundred people turned up to watch. I always tried discreetly to get on Ron's side.

I once saw him crash Tommy Smith to the deck up at Anfield. He had expertly scraped his studs down his shin, his sock was torn and blood poured from the wound. Ronnie smiled an evil self-satisfied smile, knowing that Smith would have done the same if he had managed to get his attack in first. Smith was screaming blue murder and we all turned away, not wishing to incur his wrath, but Ron just strolled past him, patting him on the head like he was a naughty schoolboy. 'You're getting soft, Tom.' (Smith, off the field, was a gentleman and entertained us well up in Liverpool.) Another time, a few seasons later, Chrissy Garland was taken off after a particularly late tackle. Ron trotted up to me. He hadn't seen who did it; he wouldn't have done, being practically blind. 'Who did it, Os?'

I told him but it was obvious that the name meant nothing. I'm sure Ron preferred *The Wheeltappers and Shunters Club* to *Match of the Day* on a Saturday night.

'The number four, Ron,' I added helpfully.

And that was that. Within five minutes both teams had used their substitutes.

Ron was proud of his hard man reputation on the field. He knew this was what he was good at and wisely, but maybe perversely, worked at his craft in the same way as others might improve their ball control or penalty-taking skills. He had no compunction at taking people out and my abiding memory of him is his walking away from writhing opposition players following a crunch that made us all think 'Ouch' with a totally blank expression on his face or a shrug of the shoulders. When I was in my early days at the club I asked him what was meant by this 'going over the top' stuff I kept hearing about. He motioned me to one side and gently rolled his foot across the ball, appearing as if to play it but revealing a boot-full of waiting studs. 'Now kick that,' he leered. It was like a hit man showing me how to load a gun.

In fact I witnessed him execute a man once. We were playing Santos, the crack Brazilian side, in a post-season friendly in Caracas, Venezuela. Keith Weller, now recovered from Ronnie's assault, scored our goal in a 4–1 defeat. The world's most famous footballer, Pele, was playing but it was a mercurial little winger on the left flank that was turning Ronnie inside out. When he scored the first goal he ran over and saluted the Brazilian fans and this really annoyed Ron. Ten minutes later the ball rolled into our area and Ron laid off long enough to encourage the boy to go for it. 'He's taken the grass,' squealed Ron. This was Harrisspeak for some poor sod falling for his wicked plan. The ensuing tackle was bone shuddering and the young wizard was taken off on a stretcher. Ron had a funny view of 'friendly' matches.

One of the big stories at the club when I first joined was about when Chelsea had played Stoke City and Ron came face to face with the most famous British footballer ever. They didn't come bigger than Stanley Matthews, but it didn't stop a young Ron Harris from larraping his legs clean out from underneath him. Poor Stan was almost 50 years of age at the time and playing out his final matches for Stoke City. Whether he really merited his first team place at this advanced age can't be certain, but if a man was putting thousands on the gate it would be hard for the club not to play him. No other player has achieved such longevity in the game at senior levels. Most players were honoured just to be on the same pitch as Matthews and at this point in his career tended to treat him like a valuable piece of china. No one would dream of hacking him down. Only Ron. At half-time a few of the older players laid into him.

'I helped him get up, didn't I?' was Ron's only defence.

'But you hurt him Ronnie, he was rolling around clutching his shins,' remonstrated one.

'Na, that wasn't me. That's his arthritis.'

It probably meant very little to Chopper but it obviously traumatised Stan, for in the autobiography he published shortly before his death, 40 years after the incident, he devoted three pages to the game.

David Webb was a real character and soon became an integral part of our little drinking firm as well as our team. We called him DJ. He was a man in a hurry and although he loved his football and his socialising he had his eye firmly on the bigger picture. He loved rubbing shoulders with the celebrities and wealthy businessmen that then, as now, gravitated towards Chelsea Football Club and sought the company of the players. Most of us loved the attention of these famous names and wealthy individuals but Webby was the only one, I think, that actually wanted to be one of them. He had tremendous energy and harnessed it by dreaming up one get rich scheme after another. Some were harebrained, but you had to admire the man for trying. It was a great source of amusement to us when Webby turned up for training.

'What d'you get up to yesterday DJ?'

'Bought a car lot.'

'Really?'

'Yeah, do you want to buy a car?'

And so on. A few of us were guilty of opening up boutiques and shops, but Webby had to be different and started up an off-the-peg wig shop in London's East End. Wigs! I ask you. Even I could have told him that purchasing a rug is an intensely personal and private thing. If DJ thought that bald men were going to walk past his shop, spot a nice toupee in the window, double back, enter the shop and buy it, then he really was inhabiting a different planet from the rest of us. The fact that his shop was sandwiched between a fish and chip shop and a minicab firm wouldn't have helped. For the opening he managed to corral a number of known faces, including the young West Ham full-back Frank Lampard and the comedian Marty Feldman. Feldman, you may remember, had very large protruding eyes and eyeballs that appeared not to like each other and stared maniacally in opposite directions. Marty Feldman made a joke at Frank Lampard's expense, but the boy came back like a comedian dealing with a heckler: 'At least when I cry the tears roll down my cheek and not down the back of my neck.'

Webby mastered handling the press to his advantage from an early stage in his career. He was forever planting stories in the papers about such and such a club being interested in him. He was a great one for raising his own profile. These transfer stories normally appeared about the time he was renegotiating his contract with the club.

Eddie McCreadie was known as Clarence because, like Ronnie, he could hardly see, Clarence being a cross-eyed lion star of TV's *Daktari*. He was always a quiet one, keeping his feelings to himself, but at the same time embracing the Kings Road culture with gusto. On one trip we realised we'd lost him only to notice him hanging upside down from the hotel balcony a few floors up. Somehow he was keeping a grip with his ankles lodged in the railings of the balcony. I rushed beneath, waiting to catch him or break his fall, whilst Webby raced up the stairs to pull him back to safety. I can't say whether his predicament was as a result of drunkenness or some half-hearted suicide attempt. Maybe it was his round next. Eddie took life too seriously even then, fretting over trivialities. Playing Southampton once he decided before the game that there were at least five players in the side that had cause to harm him because of things that had gone down in previous encounters. He overplayed it in his mind and ran out onto the pitch, putting Terry Paine on his back within seconds and despite being warned by the referee, proceeded to floor another player. We all thought he was mad but it did the trick, I suppose – no one went near him for the rest of the game.

We got off to a solid start to the 1968–69 season, and beating Manchester United, the European Cup holders, by four goals in the August sun was a great omen. It was not the first time I had played against George Best, but he was now in the stratosphere as far as stardom went. It is easy to overdo the 'players in our day' thing, but I truly believe that George, at his peak, was the best player in the world and the best player I ever saw. I don't think his like has been seen since and it may never be seen again. He and the ball were a single entity as he jigged and swerved his way goalward. Matt Busby had it about right when he held his team talks and told the others 'just give the ball to George'. Pretty deflating I imagine for his team mates, but these really were exceptional circumstances. There really was a genius in the house. I'm reminded of a schoolboy chant at the time – 'Osgood is good but Best is best'. I couldn't agree more.

Although our results were good and we were playing stylish football at that time, my game was generally quite poor and relations with the manager could have been better. Dave and I had already had a run-in before the season even kicked off when myself, Marvin, Tommy and Joe Fascione went out on the razzle after a match in Germany on the pre-season tour. At the time we stuck to a yarn about looking for Marvin's missing tooth and getting lost, but really we just got pissed. Dave found out and fined us all £50, but implied that I was the ringleader. Possibly that was the start of my strained relationship with him.

Against Burnley in the September he publicly dug me out in the dressing-room. They had beaten us courtesy of two goals from nifty winger Dave Thomas. 'Ten of you were trying out there – one wasn't,' he complained. I knew he was talking about me. He was right, but I couldn't put my finger on what was wrong, I desperately wanted to run off the ball, defend if necessary, but for some reason I didn't. Against Ipswich a couple of games later Dave substituted me for Barry Lloyd and then left me out of the team altogether. I welcomed the rest and returned home to Rose, Anthony and the ferret to contemplate. Contemplate – what? Maybe I was still in mourning for the Tommy Docherty days? Maybe I believed that I was not the player I was before I broke my leg? I don't know, but I think I was mildly depressed, and you can't always explain depression or why you get it. I was on the point of asking for a move, thinking that might reinvigorate me. I was tortured by the thought I was letting the fans down when Dave rang me and said he wanted me to try a midfield role and wear the number four shirt.

My first match in this role was against Manchester City and I revelled in it. I was fresh, enjoying picking up their forwards and bursting out of midfield to attack. I scored one, and Tommy Baldwin the other in a 2–0 win. It was the best City side in many a year and the team, managed by the avuncular Joe Mercer and coached by the charismatic Malcolm Allison, would go on to win the FA Cup at the end of the season. Colin Bell calmly controlled their midfield and Mike Summerbee weaved his way down the flank to feed bustling Francis Lee at centre-forward. I continued in my midfield role for the rest of the season and settled down well. We reached the quarter-finals of the FA Cup again, this time losing out to the holders, West Bromwich Albion, and their in-form sharp shooter, Jeff Astle. We managed to move up one place in the league at fifth and I ended the season with nine league goals – not my best tally, but I did have the excuse of being a midfield player. Reliable Bobby Tambling and Tommy Baldwin weren't doing too bad, managing 33 goals between them. Bill Shankly even made a £100,000 offer for me, doing wonders for my self-belief.

During the season Dave fined me £10 for being late for treatment one time during the season when I was injured. He knew where I was – the pub. He'd been there earlier for a bite to eat and probably spied me getting a taste for the beer. I didn't mind the fine, but couldn't understand why he, or someone at the club, saw fit to leak the story to the papers. He had first disciplined me for an incident earlier in the season not long after he took over. It was the quarter-final clash against Birmingham City at St Andrews, our old mucker Barry Bridges was playing for them, and I was having a bit of friendly banter with another of their players, Malcolm Page. At one point I told him he was getting too slow and he said, 'Shut up Osgood, you're just a wanker.'

Five minutes later I breezed past him with the ball, laid it off and then turned around and very obviously gave him the age-old wanker sign. It was a bit of fun. The crowd laughed and so did Malcolm, but although I don't think the TV cameras picked up on it, the papers did and 'Osgood's obscene gesture' was mentioned a number of times. Dave didn't fine or suspend me but he was angry and tore me off a strip. He said I was lucky not to be charged by the FA with bringing the game into disrepute. I told Dave not to worry those wankers at the FA wouldn't understand the gesture.

The thing about Peter Osgood was his absolute self-belief. If he said 'I am going to score today' or 'We will win the game,' he did and we did. Other times he said nothing. He had a great sense of his own destiny. His first touch was heavenly and he scored a better class of goal. I saw him score the same goal twice in consecutive weeks against Stoke and Leicester, and Banks and Shilton, Britain's best goalkeepers at the time. From the very edge of the box the ball was rolled to him and he fired into the top corner of the net. No looking up. Just bang, and his arm in the air almost before the ball had left his boot. He knew.

A. Hudson, Writer

7

Something in the Air

THE SUMMER OF '69 REALLY WAS A SPECIAL TIME. ASK BRYAN ADAMS. TONY Jacklin delighted us all by becoming the first British golfer to win the Open in my memory. At the Old Bailey, Justice Melford Stevenson had just sent down Ronnie and Reggie Kray for 30 years apiece and the tabloids had been salivating all summer over just whose heads they may have nailed to which floor. Concorde, a supersonic aircraft developed by the British and the French made its maiden flight, British troops had moved into Northern Ireland to control rioting in Ulster and everyone was still getting their heads around the fact that someone had somehow walked on the moon. In Hyde Park, London, the Rolling Stones staged a free concert to celebrate the life of Brian Jones, their guitarist, who had been found drowned in his swimming pool. As Mick Jagger symbolically freed thousands of white butterflies into the blue sky, the three predominant youth cults of the period jostled for attention. The Hells Angels modelled themselves on the biker gangs in the States and had taken it upon themselves to police the event. The hippies, stoned on pot and at peace with the world, were happy to be policed or were more likely unaware that they were being policed, and finally gangs of young men with cropped hair, Fred Perry T-shirts, braces, Levi jeans and Dr Marten boots skulked around the edges. These were the skinheads and their day was soon to come. Within weeks this would be the official uniform of the inhabitants of the Chelsea Shed, and just about every other football end in the country. The Rolling Stones were not top of the charts – a strange little group called Thunderclap Newman were, with a haunting song whose mood seemed to sum up the time – 'Something in the Air'.

There was something else in the air that season – me, when I scored my flying header against Leeds in the FA Cup final replay, but let's get there first. The start to the season was inauspicious. Liverpool whacked us 4–1 on the opening day and West Ham sunk us 2–0 in the next game. But we won the first home match against Ipswich Town and Ian Hutchison, now a first team regular and partnering well with Tommy and Bobby up front, scored the goal. We then remained unbeaten for the next eight games. I was still playing from the midfield but managing to get on the score sheet regularly, and as the season wore on drifted back into my old attacking role and the number nine shirt. The team was gelling nicely. Peter Bonetti in goal was simply getting better and better and reaching his peak. The Cat, or Catty, as we knew him, was an acrobatic keeper who if it hadn't been for a surplus of excellent goalies in the period would have been the England number one choice. Catty was never one to go out on the town. It just wasn't his scene. We used to tease him, saying he was a tightwad, but he was a few years older than us and had a different social and family life. He was on a quest for perfection, was Catty. He'd be first in training and last to leave. Even conceding in practice seemed to upset him. I have nothing but admiration for the man. His surname, it won't surprise you, means 'keeper of the castle'.

The defence and midfield were superb and were now working together like a well-oiled machine – Ron, Eddie, Demps and Marvin, and Holly and Houseman – Hollins, a skilful, dedicated footballer who had already gained an England cap, and Peter, who was quietly effective wherever he played. Webby by now was truly establishing himself and his pugilistic demeanour and sense of humour had already endeared him to the crowd. Tommy, Charlie, Alan Birchenall, Hutch and myself were all doing the business up front.

Then a 17 year old literally ambled across to the ground from his home in the prefabs just across the Fulham Road. Prefabs (short for prefabricated houses) were the temporary accommodation put up by the government after the Second World War to house families displaced by bombing and replenish the public housing stock. There are very few prefabs left now, 50 years on, but for many big city families the notion that the accommodation was temporary was laughable after they'd lived in them for 20-odd years. Alan's prefab was a happy home with his extended family coming in and out all day long. His mum and dad had great taste – their dog was named Ossie.

Alan Hudson was a self-confident, good-looking young lad who wore his hair long and his shirts loud. He was what they called in those days a face, and his looks were such that he would not have been out of place plucking an electric guitar in the popular Mod band the Small Faces. Even though a boy amongst men, the fact that he truly was a Chelsea boy (he could have walked into the Shed and been on first-name terms with most of the local lads in there) and that it was obvious that he was exceptionally skilful and talented, meant he was no shrinking violet and he soon became a leading light in our set. We palled up almost immediately, him showing me the drinking dens up and down the Kings Road that I may have missed so far and introducing me to the web of eccentric characters that seemed to form the fabric of Kings Road and World's End society. I invited him to come rabbiting with me, but he always made excuses. Can't imagine why. We shared the same attitude then to football, authority, drink and women, and in the end we shared a destiny.

Once he established himself in the first team Huddy's arrival was catching everyone's eye. Alf Ramsey picked him for the England Under-23s, and we were to play in the same game. This was one of the few occasions when he asked me for advice.

'Just look after yourself, Huddy. Don't worry about me, or anyone else up front. No one is going to worry about you.'

'I can't play like that,' protested Alan. And he couldn't, for Alan was a generously creative player. His whole game was about creating space, opportunities and making passes that would make his peers drool. But that is how those Under-23 games were, with every single player desperate to impress Sir Alf Ramsey and showcase themselves. They were missing the point, as by now they should have realised that Alf valued other qualities above individual flair. I think it was that game when Brian Kidd shot at every opportunity, sometimes from 40 yards out. Mind you, he did score, but Alf was obviously not over-impressed, for Kidd got even less caps than I did and that's saying something. 'See what you mean,' sighed Huddy after the game.

It was at another game between the English and Scottish Leagues that to my surprise Alf produced some scotch and encouraged us all to have a slug 'to put fire in our bellies and to fight the cold'. I certainly did, and big John McGrath the Southampton player took the bottle and swigged away as you would a can of Coke on a hot summer's day. I'm sure he played that game half-pissed. He rolled his sleeves up, swayed out onto the pitch and proceeded to kick lumps out of the talented Rangers forward Colin Stein.

Alf Ramsey has rarely been credited with having a sense of humour, but he did. One time when I was staying at Hendon Hall and stepping off the coach for morning training he greeted me with 'Well, Ossie, how do you fancy training today?'

'Not a lot, Alf,' I unwisely but truthfully replied.

'Well, you're going to fucking well enjoy it!' he told me in those clipped, plummy tones. I was shocked. It was like catching the Queen kicking one of the corgis up the arse.

One Sunday evening in February 1970, I had a call from Dave Sexton at home. I was a bit annoyed to have to come to the phone as I was engrossed in *Songs of Praise* on the TV, but Dave had the news that Alf had been in touch and wanted me to report to the England camp in Brussels. The senior international side were out there for a match against Belgium. I was not particularly excited, because I knew that Martin Chivers and Rodney Marsh were already in Belgium to deputise for Bobby Charlton, who'd had to pull out. I said to Dave that what with the hamstring injury I was trying to shake off and the fact that I'd only be carrying the bags anyway, I'd give it a miss.

'Give it a miss? Give it a miss?' Sexton was almost speechless. 'Look Ossie, I'm not supposed to tell you this but Alf has told me you will definitely play on Wednesday night.'

I ran out into the garden, leapt the hedge and didn't stop running till I reached Heathrow Airport.

When I arrived the press boys were waiting and posed back-page photos followed, typical of the period: me, Marsh and Martin Chivers all smiling broadly and pointing to one another, indicating we each thought that the other was playing. Those tabloid photos, often taken by top snapper Monty Fresco, seem so dated today. Players dressed up as the Lone Ranger or with crutches and parrots on their shoulders to support some tenuous link with the story. I can't see Roy Keane, David Beckham or Gianfranco Zola going along with too much of that these days.

Naturally, I didn't mention to the others that I knew it was me who would be playing. I can't imagine that Alf had told the others the same thing. He even winked at me at one point; his behaviour was sometimes strange. The conditions were terrible, but we overcame the snow as well as Belgium to win 3–1 and I was delighted with my game. Pulling on the England shirt gave me goose bumps and I felt overwhelmed for one of the few times in my career. I thought of my family at home and felt little pangs behind my eyeballs. The brickie from Windsor running out for England. Who'd have thought it? Not me.

I played well and was totally at home with the occasion and the team. To me it seemed absolutely natural that I should be here and I fully expected that this was the beginning of a long and fruitful international career. I had just turned 23 and the time seemed right. Alan Ball scored 2 goals that evening, which was some achievement considering that in his other 71 appearances he managed only another 6. Me, Bobby Moore and Bally went out in Brussels that night and got very pissed. The club we found was dimly lit. Bobby went to the bar and me and Bally looked around. 'What do you notice about this place?' whispered Bally. I looked around and picked up on the fact that there were no women anywhere.

'Shortage of ladies?' I volunteered. Bally nodded over to a nearby table, where two young chaps were clearly necking. I was shocked, I have to admit. Country boy and all that. I knew homosexuality existed, I can remember calling people 'Mo' at school, a long-forgotten shortening of the word 'homosexual' which was common currency when I was a kid. But I had never knowingly come across a gay man. This was 1970 and the '60s – the decade of sexual liberation – had come and gone, but the sexual liberation they referred to was all of the heterosexual variety. Naturally one or two of us had our suspicions about Liberace, but that was as far as it went. We looked up to the bar to see how Bobby was getting on. He had obviously drawn the same conclusion and had decided to do something to crack us up. And he did – he was standing erect at the bar, straight-faced, making his order, but had dropped his strides to his feet. The sight of his legs and Y-fronts was causing much excitement around him. There was no topping that. All in all, it was a wonderful night.

That team still contained the core of the 1966 World Cup-winning side and they were good, make no mistake. Bobby Moore as captain patrolled the middle of the park, quietly but surely. It was like having your dad out there with you. He made you feel safe; everything would be fine because Bobby was there. I remember Dave Sexton once berating me for allowing Bobby to take the ball from me every time in a league match against the Hammers. As you moved forward at Bobby he would drop back and back in such a relaxed way, with his arms dangling, that eventually you'd relax and only then would he nip forward and snatch the ball from you. Alan Ball, too, running everywhere, a real human dynamo, creating space and then Martin Peters reading the game and laying on perceptive passes as if he had access to some fast-forward switch in his brain, and dependable Geoff Hurst alongside to play off. These guys allowed me in and I felt like a made man when Alf came up to me after the game and rested his hand on my shoulder. 'Well done, son, and welcome to the fold.' It had taken four years since first making an England full squad but now I was in. Could my season get any better?

Yes, it could. We couldn't stop winning in the League, with me and Hutch firing on all cylinders. We were disposing of the top sides with ease and aplomb, outplaying them with entertaining, stylish and fun football – just how I liked it. We defeated Arsenal and Manchester City at the Bridge, beat Manchester United at Old Trafford and demolished Crystal Palace 5–1 at Selhurst Park. I remember the game well because I scored four goals and we had a riot as Charlie Cooke tore their defence to shreds. Every time I shot it seemed to be bang on target. It was Christmas time and Chelsea fans swelled Selhurst to its limits, but the atmosphere was celebratory and euphoric, as if the crowd knew we were accelerating now toward something big. 'Jingle bells, Jingle bells, Jingle all the way, Oh what fun it is to see, Chelsea win away,' they sang. Charlie Cooke took his game seriously, but never himself. He wasn't into the star thing at all, very conscious, I think, that playing professional football was going to form a relatively small part of his life – not define it. I think it was that day against Palace when he sharpened the studs on his football boots to points so as to get a better grip on the hard pitch, and how well it worked – he should have patented the idea. Charlie also had the best engine I've ever seen on a footballer.

There was a sharp interruption to our form when Leeds United thrashed us 5–2 at Stamford Bridge. Leeds were the League champions and had a reputation, among players at least, as being the dirtiest side in the First Division. They thought they were just ultra-competitive, but it went beyond that. Brian Clough, Derby County's outspoken young manager, famously took Don Revie to task with this accusation on *Match of the Day* and Revie struggled to defend himself. They were a larger-than-life team, with larger-than-life players like Billy Bremner, Jack Charlton, Norman Hunter, Peter Lorimer and Johnny Giles. When such luminaries protesting a decision surrounded a referee or demanded a penalty many of them couldn't fail to be intimidated. But they didn't intimidate us in the slightest, and that's why they hated us.

They disliked our Kings Road image, our camaraderie, our flair and our lack of respect. We had already beaten them in the League Cup this season but in their arrogance I'm sure they would have maintained they had no interest in that competition. Bigger fish to fry and all that.

Meanwhile we had knocked out Birmingham City in the third round of the FA Cup, a team that fielded our old colleagues Tony Hateley and Bert Murray. We bounced back from Leeds to wallop Arsenal 3-0 at Highbury, where a gangly, long-haired boy named Charlie George came on as a substitute. Charlie was rough and ready and would take no shit from anyone. The bad boys in the game soon thought twice about hacking him. One of the first things he said to me was 'I'll see you in the tunnel after, Osgood,' in those unmistakable flat tones of his. Also in the Gunners side was Peter Marinello, who the press had built up as the new George Best. He was Scottish, not Irish, coming to London from Hibernian, but had the hair, the clothes, the looks but, unfortunately, not the talent of George Best. No one did. How pleased the media were to knock him down again.

Burnley and Palace went in the fourth and fifth rounds of the competition and then we faced Queens Park Rangers in the quarter-finals. QPR were another side that enjoyed their football and played in a crowd-pleasing style. Rodney Marsh was a great individualist and showman but actually running the show down there, on the pitch (and probably off it) was Terry Venables. Up front with Marsh was the man I replaced in the Chelsea side – Barry Bridges. The game was a real thriller at Loftus Road in which we triumphed 4–2. I bagged a hat trick of goals, and Terry and Barry got the goals for Rangers.

We were drawn against Watford, Third Division giant-killers, in the semi-final and to be honest we were all pretty confident that our place at Wembley was assured. The tie was to be played at a neutral ground and White Hart Lane was selected as the venue. Most Chelsea fans do not harbour neutral feelings about Tottenham Hotspur, but we often got a good result there so it suited us fine. Sure enough, we scored in the opening minutes when Dave Webb steamed up the pitch and slammed home a nod-down from John Dempsey. The floodgates had opened, or so we thought, but in a pattern that has become only too familiar to Chelsea fans up to the present day when we are up against lesser opposition – we conceded almost straight away. Watford then found their feet and contained us well for the remainder of the first half. At half-time we were demoralised for losing the lead and not taking this small side apart. Dave Sexton could see we were over-doing it and bucked us up. By the time the buzzer went to get back out on the pitch we were revitalised and confident again in our own superiority. From the start of the second half we were on top and when I rose to a Peter Houseman cross and nodded the ball into the net we knew we were going to take them apart. Peter himself scored next, and then Hutch let rip with a searing left-footer to make the score 4–1. Houseman, in one of his best games ever, tied it all up by scoring the fifth and final goal. Hutch too had come so far. From the nervous kid only months before he was now terrorising defences with his strong attacking play and I could really see him playing for England. We were a group of players all reaching our personal peaks simultaneously – always a good recipe for the most successful and memorable teams.

Leeds United were to be our opponents in the FA Cup final and nothing could have pleased us more. There was no other club on the planet we would enjoy beating so much, and I am sure the feeling was mutual. If motivation plays a key part in these things then we had it in bucketloads. Everyone wanted to beat them, not because they were the best, but because just about everyone outside of Leeds just didn't like them. They were so far up their own arses it was untrue. There was a terrace chant at the time and you heard it wherever you went:

> We all hate Leeds,
> and Leeds, and Leeds,
> Leeds and Leeds, and Leeds and Leeds,
> We all fucking hate Leeds.

The rich lyrics smacked of Greenaway. Only for Leeds did Chopper get the iodine out and smear his studs.

Firstly, though, there was the small matter of the League Championship to deal with. Everton were steaming away with it, with us, Leeds and Derby grouped together just behind. When we lost 5–2 at Goodison Park we knew any chance of being champions were dashed, but second or third was still a reality. Everton had a smart side with goalie Gordon West, along with Peter Bonetti, vying to be Gordon Banks' deputy in the England goal, Howard Kendall, Brian Labone and Colin Harvey in the middle of the park and Joe Royle, the target man, with Alan Ball and Alan Whittle working away for him. Whittle was a little guy, with white curly hair – 'Five foot two, Eyes of blue, Alan Whittle's after you' – went the chant. Losing to West Bromwich Albion the following week put paid to our second position hopes and we ended the season finishing third. Still, this was again an improvement on the previous season and our equal best finish since the historic 1955 season. The game against Albion, however, was more significant because young Alan Hudson fell badly and somehow broke his ankle. He was out for the final and any hopes of forcing himself into Alf Ramsey's 1970 World Cup Squad could be forgotten. I knew how he felt, just arriving as a 17 year old in a sizzling team, forcing the country to take notice only to be hacked down before he'd even got into his stride, missing a cup final that he should have been playing in.

Three years after our defeat to Spurs we were back at Wembley for another FA Cup final. This time I was definitely playing. The big news at the time was the break-up of The Beatles. They hadn't played live for years and were displaying signs of madness – John Lennon had disposed of a perfectly pretty and sane wife and taken up with Yoko Ono, for example – but the country was shocked that the mop-top dream really was over. Simon and Garfunkel's 'Bridge Over Troubled Water' floated over the airwaves of the nation. Everyone I knew came to Wembley – Mum, Dad and dozens of friends and family. Every other player was the same. The pitch was a quagmire due to the fact that someone had stupidly allowed it to be used for the Horse of the Year Show only days before. Norman Hunter tried to psyche Hutch out by running alongside him and whispering, 'You're only in the team because of your silly long throw.' That was Leeds for you. But Hutch replied in the best possible way by promptly scoring with a diving header. Ronnie Harris was also a giant that day, he was carrying a hamstring injury and only played courtesy of a cortisone injection, yet he lifted us all and held us together when we looked like we might crumble. When the chips were down the real leader in him emerged.

Big Jack Charlton had put Leeds into the lead. It was a bad goal from our point of view – all goals against you are bad, but this one seemed to roll between Eddie McCreadie and Ron Harris and into the net while they looked on as if a small dog in the park was trotting past them. But then our equaliser was just as embarrassing for Leeds. Peter Houseman hit a low drive from 20 yards and somehow Gary Sprake in the Leeds goal let it pass beneath him. Tap-backs from his defenders Reaney and Cooper had approached him with more speed and spin. Sprake was a bit of an anomaly in that Leeds team. I rarely saw him have a great game and his howlers were often aired on *The Big Match* and *Match of the Day*. Don Revie, always striving for perfection, must have known that there were better prospects than Sprake around, yet he persisted with him. Very strange. I secretly wondered whether the Welsh goalkeeper was Revie's love child. We stayed at one each until seven minutes from the end, when Mick Jones tucked away a rebound from an Allan Clarke shot that hit the post. Catty was left floundering and the rest of us thought that was it. So near, yet so far. Then just before the end, that man again, Ian Hutchinson, saved the day. He braved Jack Charlton's flying boot and headed home. Dave Sexton's faith in this boy had been lavishly rewarded and I felt ashamed for ever thinking the guy was not a great player.

The prospect of extra time pained us. We dropped to the floor, some of us rolling around clutching our legs with cramp. We had survived. We were still in it but we didn't relish the next half-hour. Dave Sexton was at his best though, and he made a rallying speech: 'You've got 'em now. Look at them. They thought they had it and we snatched it from them. Their heads are down. You're in the driving seat, believe me.'

Extra time was something of an anti-climax as both teams were exhausted and giving nothing away, but I think if Dave hadn't geed us up in the way he did Leeds would have gone straight through us in that added period. Although it has happened a few times since, this was to be the first FA Cup final replay in Wembley's history. At the end of the game both teams did a lap of honour together for the fans, a somewhat hypocritical act of solidarity bearing in mind the animosity that simmered between us. But we felt that we had both endured something special and it seemed a natural thing to do.

One thing about us Chelsea players was that we didn't allow rivalry and playing grudges to spill over from the pitch to the players' bar or any social venue. We would normally be first at the bar and first to buy the drinks. If there was to be any arguing or fisticuffs it would be between ourselves, just like any group of mates, and not against our opposite numbers. We had our reputation as social animals and we liked to live up to it. Many a time we'd be discussing which nightclub or pub to move on to when players from other teams would be shaking their heads and wondering why we were not going home to our wives. Or, in some cases, worrying that some of us might be going home to *their* wives.

Old Trafford was the venue for the replay in the middle of the week 18 days after the Wembley clash. Hardly a neutral venue, with Leeds being far closer to Manchester than we were, but you would never have known. Manchester was teeming with blue and white; it seemed the whole of west London and the Home Counties had downed tools and headed up the M1. An army had arrived and we were the vanguard. Leeds piled on the early pressure and nearly scored on a few occasions. Ronnie was put on Eddie Gray, who had caused so many problems for our Eddie Mac in the previous match, and that turned out to be a masterstroke, as the brilliant Scottish winger was never allowed to get into gear. But they still managed to maintain the pressure and eventually big Mick Jones screamed a shot past Catty and we filed in for half-time 1–0 down. In the dressing-room it was all battle talk. We didn't need lifting. It was all what they had done to us, and what we would do to them. There was a myth at the time that Jackie Charlton had a little black book with the names of players in, players he was waiting to damage in some way. 'When I score,' I said to anyone that might have been listening, 'I'm going to rip his black book off him and laugh in his face as I write my name in it.'

I doubt there ever was a black book, and if there was it certainly wouldn't be in the pocket of his shorts. We had no pockets.

'Don't worry about Charlton Os, he's just a wanker with a long neck,' said Hutch.

He hated Leeds with a passion and detested Charlton.

The second half was even more physical, with Bremner, Hunter and Charlton crunching their way around the pitch. When Leeds forced a corner, Charlton would lumber forward and create havoc in the penalty area in the hope that Leeds could scramble in one of their pretty goals in the confusion. Hutch used the cover of that confusion to kick Big Jack right up the arse and got away with it. He couldn't retaliate because the referee was watching, but if looks could kill Hutch would have been riddled with machine-gun bullets. I'm sure the big man walked back down the field muttering, 'I must remember to put that impertinent fellow's name in my black book when I get home.'

What followed was a goal that, if not the best of my career, was the one that mattered more than any other. I picked the ball up from Johnny Hollins on the halfway line and made a run to the right, then slid the ball to Hutch who careered off in the opposite direction. Big Jack chased him and left a gap in the middle. Charlie Cooke loomed up and Hutch passed inside to him. I was still running, and Charlie saw me and chipped the ball precisely into my current. At that point I knew I was going to score; you just know these things. What happened then was as near to an out-of-body experience as I have ever had. I saw myself in the air bulleting towards the ball like a heat-seeking missile. The ball seemed to hang there waiting for me until my head and it collided perfectly. My eyes locked on the crowd behind the goal and I could see the faces – real features and expressions, not just the blur of the crowd – and I knew exactly whereabouts the ball was going to smack the back of the net. In the split second I hit the ball I also knew David Harvey the keeper would be helpless (what happened to Sprake? Did he drop his rail ticket to Manchester?). Absolutely sweet.

But there was still a match to win and we had been here before. The fans took over. I have never witnessed anything like it, before or since. They started chanting – *Chelsea, Chelsea* – in a trance-like fashion and it got louder and louder, and continued throughout the remainder of the 90 minutes and the extra time that followed. It lifted us further and disorientated Leeds, whose fans were either drowned out by the sheer volume or had fallen under the hypnotic qualities of the chant and the mood. Now there were 12 of us: the 11 players and the crowd. Leeds had no chance. Hutch chucked in one of his marvellous throws and it brushed Charlton's head, but Webby was up and he headed home. We had won the Cup!

It's such a shame that I can't remember everything that happened after. I can't remember how it felt except that it was so, so good. I would love to have been able to bottle that feeling, that atmosphere, those minutes and every now and then open the bottle and just feel it again. But you can't. I do remember that Tommy Baldwin and I swapped shirts with a couple of the Leeds boys and when we went up to collect our winners' medals the official wouldn't give them to us, thinking we were on the losing side. Victory was sweet though, I know that. Sweeter still when I heard that Jackie Charlton had left the building. Literally. He is the only man ever not to go up to collect his loser's medal and apparently walked straight out of Old Trafford and jumped in a cab, such was his disgust and anger. That really made our day.

I remember standing on the terraces below the Bovril bar in the Shed end with my dad. Osgood picked the ball up on the halfway line, beat a couple of Tottenham players and sent a screamer into the top of the net. The ground erupted and Ossie, the King of Stamford Bridge, stood and milked the adulation. My dad shook his head and smiled. 'He's a bit special, ain't he son?'

Just before the end of the game Chopper Harris slightly over-stroked a pass to Ossie. If he had wanted to he could have run and kept the ball in play, but he just stood there, hands on hips, and glared at Harris.

'You're a lazy fucker Osgood,' shouted the old man, 'get your arse in gear.'

Thirty years later I recount this memory to Ossie as we work on this book. 'Perhaps your dad was right,' he muses. 'My dad said the same thing. Bless him.' He tells me his dad died a few years back as did mine. He raises his glass and says, 'Here's to your dad and my dad. I bet they're up there somewhere, looking down saying, "Look at those two still talking bollocks".'

M. King, Writer and Scrap Metal Dealer

8

Mexican Waves

AFTER THE GAME WE ALL CRAMMED TOGETHER ON CLOUD NINE AND FLOATED off to a Manchester nightclub. I can't remember too much about it except that I did meet a lovely young blonde lady who had joined our company. Her name escapes me, just as she did a few hours later. I told her I'd just won the FA Cup and she became caught up in my euphoria. She agreed to accompany me back to my hotel room. I couldn't believe how this wonderful night was shaping up. I was trying to act cool and collected as I turned the key but to my horror when the door opened all I could see was bodies everywhere. It was like that Marx Brothers film where scores of people crush into a tiny room. These were my mates from Windsor and elsewhere, snoring, farting and vomiting. My pretty blonde turned to me and smiled. She stood on tiptoe and kissed my cheek. 'Another time.'

We all got the train home in the morning from Manchester Piccadilly, bleary-eyed players and fans alike, all of whom had spent the night partying. We celebrated more all the way back to London and when we alighted at Euston there was a large crowd of fans to meet us. The scenes were incredible but what sticks in my mind most is the sight of two very old Chelsea pensioners at the front of the crowd in their full red and black regalia. One was supporting himself with a stick and as I got close I shook his hand and noticed he was crying. I realised then how much this cup win meant to so many people.

Interest in me as a business proposition was stepping up. All sorts of people seemed to want a piece of Peter Osgood, and I had the problem (wish I had that problem now!) of what to do with my money. The perceived wisdom, at least from the people who were trying to get you to part with it, was that to leave cash in the bank was almost criminal. I opened a boutique in Mitcham, south London, which with hindsight was almost as pointless as opening an Oddbins in Saudi Arabia. Boutique was the new name for clothes shops, another stupid French word like discotheque that was supposed to suggest it was more than it actually was. We got our clothes from a man in Chelsea. Were probably paying retail prices for them for all I knew. Even though we had a big crowd for the opening, all of those people and everyone they knew made a point of giving our shop a wide berth. The boutique closed after 18 months due to lack of interest, especially mine. George Best had launched a boutique, with Mike Summerbee if I remember correctly; I probably got the idea from that. I was certainly encouraged by George's success with his own range of football boots and had high hopes when I put my name to a specific boot. I think they lasted a bit longer than the boutique, but not much. Meanwhile Peter Bonetti's branded goalkeepers' gloves had cornered the market.

Some of the lads had agents to look after their business interests and maximise their earnings, so I thought maybe it was time I trusted my business affairs to someone who understood them better than I. Beyond starting up a building firm with Dad and brother Mick it was all a different world. They weren't agents as we know them today. No one negotiated with the club on your behalf; they simply attempted to get you deals such as advertising, branding, appearances and the like. I ended up trying a few. With one we formed a limited company and as far as I knew we were raking it in. Therefore I was curious when my bank manager asked me to come in and see him. Even I knew that if I was being summoned something was up. I didn't have to go far, as I used the Fulham Broadway branch of this particular bank. My manager revealed that Peter Osgood Ltd was £1,500 in the red and wondered how I planned to rectify this. So did I. £1,500 represented the equivalent of a couple of months of my wages as a player and money should have been accumulating in this account, not haemorrhaging out. He took me through the transactions on the accounts and I sunk lower and lower in the chair as I read of purchases of TVs, furniture and expensive meals and wine. Ossie had been had. I wasn't the first and I won't be the last, but maybe the FA or the clubs should have had some sort of register of reputable business representatives. We were young naïve men after all, not businessmen wise to the ways of the world – the very reason these parasites homed in on us in the first place.

Still, my domestic finances were looking better. We sold our house in Windsor for £8,000 and bought a lovely house in Tadworth, Surrey for £16,000. My second son Mark had come along by now and we wanted something bigger. Tadworth was closer to Stamford Bridge and the Mitcham training ground. We lived on the edge of Epsom Downs, a beautiful landmark and home of the Derby racecourse.

FA Cup-winners, third in the league, my first England cap and 35 goals. I had also scored in every round of the FA Cup including the final, a record that has not been repeated since. Not a bad season, but imagine my delight when Alf Ramsey named me in his England squad. I knew I was hot and felt confident that I could play my part in helping England retain the World Cup in Mexico. After my debut against Belgium and Alf's welcoming me to the fold I was disappointed that our Cup replay against Leeds had disqualified me from playing the next game against Wales in the Home Internationals. But I was baffled when Alf didn't select me for the two other remaining Home International games. It was generally agreed that I was at the top of my form and the papers were screaming for my inclusion. This worried me a little because it crossed my mind that it might make Alf go the other way. He was not one to bow to media pressure. I was understandably relieved, then, to be named in the Mexico squad, but by no means confident now that I would be in the team.

Alf's preparation was second to none. We met at Hendon Hall near to Wembley to bond and get to understand the programme. Alf, Harold Shepherdson, the trainer, and we, the squad, were all confident that we would win the World Cup, but Alf was taking no chances. He was taking personal charge of our diets, our fitness, our frame of mind and everything else. On the last night before flying from Heathrow to Mexico we had a dinner at Whites Hotel near Hyde Park where each player was presented with a silver salver from the London Sporting Club. We all looked a picture in our specially made suits and gleaming smiles. Indeed, we *were* a picture – in the following day's papers.

After Alf had reccied the hotel in Mexico City, we settled in and I shared a room with Geoff Hurst and Jeff Astle. By now I knew Geoff Hurst reasonably well. He was a steady sort of a bloke, very often on the telephone to his wife. Nothing wrong with that, except that Judith his wife was in the same hotel, and Geoff seemed preoccupied over where she was at any given time. Astle was more up my chimney; I had seen him on the plane on the way over knocking back the miniatures, safely out of the vision of Alf Ramsey.

One of our first matches was a friendly against Colombia and we were to stay in the best (maybe the only?) hotel in Bogota. On the steps of the hotel we were assaulted by culture shock. Policeman or soldiers, it was hard to tell which, loitered around with large guns hanging around their necks or from their waists, and young children scampered around begging and scavenging. One little boy sat pathetically next to a bowl with a stump protruding from his raggedy, short trousers where one of his legs should have been. Someone told us, and I don't know whether this was true, that some parents in this country actually destroyed limbs in order to give their children an edge in the begging stakes. Stranger things have happened – wasn't it a Colombian footballer that was murdered a few years back for an unsatisfactory performance in the World Cup?

Booking 34 people in at reception was an organisational nightmare, even for Alf who prided himself on having covered every last detail, so a few of us placed our bags on the floor and began to explore the foyer area. Bobby Moore and Bobby Charlton drifted into a small jewellery shop attached to the hotel and I followed them in. It was pokey and cheap-looking with nothing that seemed worth buying, let alone pinching. The merchandise reminded me of the old rubbish that would be inside one of those grabber machines found on the end of English seaside piers when I was a lad. We filed out and rejoined the throng. Suddenly it was pandemonium. A small, dusky dark-haired lady who I recognised from behind the counter in the jewellers was shouting and screaming, pointing at Bobby Moore. Poor Bob looked puzzled. I think he even looked behind him over his shoulder at one stage, like in the films. We could tell she was claiming that Bobby had put something in his pocket and by the signs she was making, she was saying it was a bracelet. The police arrived quickly on the scene and Bobby was very publicly searched. He remained totally calm throughout, though we all became more and more concerned. Naturally they found nothing on Bob's person but they were either dissatisfied or determined to be awkward, as they arrested him and took him away for questioning. Here we were in a strange country, a very strange country, where being English counted for nothing, the people were obviously mad and our captain and one of the most famous men in the world was being marched off, who knows where. Sir Alf followed, looking more worried than I had ever seen him.

Mooro was kept under house arrest at the British Embassy and we had to return to Mexico City. Jimmy Greaves famously climbed the embassy wall and literally dropped in to see him, and reported that he was in good spirits. Eventually no charges were brought, and Bobby was freed and allowed to rejoin us all back in Mexico.

That was about it. Yet ever since the incident has been subject to all sorts of conspiracy theories: it was a plot to destabilise the Cup-holders by the Government of Mexico or another interested party, Bobby did nick it, someone else nicked it – I've heard them all. Recently on a TV documentary about the life of Bobby Moore the respected sports writer Jeff Powell revealed that Bobby had confided to him that one of the young players in the squad had stolen the bracelet, and Bobby knew it but wouldn't grass. Jeff even claimed he knew the identity of the thief. In the same programme Rodney Marsh confirmed the story; Mooro had told him too. He too knows the identity of the thief, but will not disclose it. Young player? In the jeweller's shop? Do they mean me?

Complete and utter bollocks! There are four possible answers to the mystery – Bobby Moore nicked it, Bobby Charlton nicked it, I (or someone else in the shop we didn't notice) nicked it, or there was no theft. I know it wasn't me. I was young and some might say reckless, but I was not short of money. The notion that I got off the coach, walked almost immediately into a jewellery shop and lifted a bracelet in view of the England captain and the other most respected footballer in the country is ridiculous. I'm convinced it wasn't Mooro and Bobby Charlton wouldn't even nick himself shaving, which leaves me to conclude there was no bracelet.

I don't subscribe to the destabilisation theories either. The manageress was an excitable nutcase – that's my take. A group of foreign men walk into her shop, grunt a few times and then walk out again. She looks down and sees that her prize item is missing. Her South American blood is boiling and she runs out and confronts who she thinks is the culprit. Later she finds the bracelet; she had forgotten that she had moved it to one side to give it a clean. She can't possibly admit it to anyone, not after the fuss it has caused. Or maybe it was a frame up, a try-on to squeeze money out of some wealthy Europeans. Who knows? On that same TV documentary Tina, Bobby's first wife, dismissed the theory. She said Bob would have confided in her if this had been the case. I'm sure he would have confided in Tina before Rodney Marsh, that's for sure, or his close friends like Geoff Hurst, Martin Peters and Jimmy Greaves. But there you go; I don't take anything Marsh says too seriously. But why Jeff Powell, a man I admire for his integrity, would say it baffles me. I shall have to ask him when I see him.

Anyway, with all that behind us we attempted to get back to the reality of winning the World Cup. We opened our Guadalajara group campaign on 2 June against Romania (it was the first time they had been allowed in the competition) and I was one of the substitutes. We won 1–0 through a Geoff Hurst goal and I came on for Franny Lee. I felt I made my mark and had a good game. The next match was to be five days later against an ominous-looking Brazil who'd already crushed Czechoslovakia, from our group, by four goals to one. Besides the legendary Pele, other Brazilians like Jairzinho, Rivelino and Tostao had emerged from under the great man's shadow. We were getting the English papers a day or two late but I was heartened to see there was a bit of a campaign to play me against Brazil. Tommy Docherty had demanded it all over the back page of one of the tabloids. Meanwhile, we had a practice match with the A team playing the Bs, so to speak. I was spearheading the B side and played an absolute blinder, running rings around our defenders, nutmegging Nobby Stiles, displaying confident ball control – the lot – and all in front of the manager. Later that day Mooro confided in me. 'Alf has asked me whether I think you're ready and I told him that you must play. Ossie, you're in, don't worry about that.'

'Thanks Bob, that's tremendous.' This would be my biggest stage so far – playing up front for England against Brazil in the World Cup. The two greatest sides in the world. Whoever won this match would go on to win the Cup, surely, and if it was us and I played my part I could be there, in the final, finding the net. How much better could life get? In the same way I knew that my header in the FA Cup final was a goal before it reached the net, I knew that I would make the difference against Brazil. I was overwhelmed by my sense of destiny.

At the team meeting I was all ears, desperate to hear the confirmation of my inclusion. Hearing it from Mooro was good enough, but you never really knew with Alf. As I said before, he moved in mysterious ways. 'The team to face Brazil will be the same team that finished against Romania,' he eventually announced.

Phew, I'm in! I thought. I grinned over at Bobby and he flashed a smile back and unfolded his thumb to me. Suddenly, though, Alf was saying something about Franny coming in near post. Bobby looked confused. I was worried. Bob raised his arm. 'Excuse me Alf, you're talking about Francis, but Ossie came on for Francis and he finished the game against the Romanians.'

Alf looked at me. His expression said it all. 'Oh, I'm ever so sorry Ossie,' he said and then calmly resumed the team talk. I was not even named in the squad of 16! I was devastated and wanted to walk out there and then but I felt paralysed. Now I had an inkling of how Jimmy Greaves felt when he was left out of the 1966 World Cup final. Another of Alf's strange decisions. I know it turned out for the best, but Roger Hunt over Jimmy Greaves? No disrespect, but there was no contest.

That evening, against all the rules, I hurried out of the hotel alone and hit the first bar I could find, and then the next and the next. I got myself paralytic with drink and have only vague memories of sharing my misery with groups of England fans that were out there for the finals. What they thought, God knows. Quite early in the evening I remember drowning my sorrows with one particular England supporter. 'Alf's got to start playing wingers,' he slurred, 'all that talent going to waste.'

I nodded encouragingly.

'Take your own Charlie Cooke,' he went on. 'Why Alf has never played him defies belief.'

'He's Scottish,' I pointed out.

The man went silent for a minute.

'No, I don't think it's that. I'm sure it's because he's a winger.'

In the morning I would not get out of bed, despite the appeals of the two Jeffs, and missed training. Alf tried to see me but I shouted at the door, 'Go away. Don't say a word. You can't excuse what you have done to me – you slaughtered me in front of the entire squad – just leave me alone!' He did. Later Harold Shepherdson, the trainer and a caring, considerate man, came and sat with me and soaked up my disappointment, anger and misery. He just listened and I felt a whole lot better.

Ironically, Alf brought Francis Lee off in the Brazil game after the inevitable Jairzinho goal had seen them one up by the turn. He also brought off Bobby Charlton, reasoning I guess that by introducing Jeff Astle alongside Geoff Hurst (at least two-thirds of our room got a game!) we could beat the Brazilians in the air. All they did was close off the flow of crosses coming in and the score stayed as it was. The highlight of the game was Gordon Banks' reflex save from Pele's header. Gordon was covering his near post when Pele forcefully headed the ball towards the opposite corner. Pele spun around, convinced he had scored, but somehow Banks flung himself the width of the goal and miraculously turned the ball away with his fingertips.

Another five days saw us play the last group game against Czechoslovakia and me sitting on the bench once again. An Allan Clarke penalty saw us through and, as against Romania, I came on replacing Astle and again it was generally thought I played well. Not in Alf's eyes, obviously, because I was not to be part of what followed: the notorious quarter-final clash with the West Germans in Leon. Even though England had lost to Brazil we got out of the group in second place.

Much has been said and written about what went wrong in that Germany game, which appeared to be in the bag after Alan Mullery from six yards and Martin Peters ghosting in at the far post had seen England two up at half-time. Helmut Schoen had shown a perceptive grasp of the use of substitutes during the Germans' group games, and after 57 minutes brought on the winger Grabowski to run and harry our sweltering defence. Beckenbauer beat Mullery and fired from a distance, and the ball seemed to bounce under Peter Bonetti's body to roll into the net. Poor Catty, he had stepped in for Gordon Banks who may have taken ice in a drink – he succumbed to the dreaded trots – and because of this one mistake was lampooned and victimised by the English nation for many years after. It must have affected his confidence. Brian Labone, the Everton centre-half, slated Catty there and then, which was unfair and unhelpful, but tensions were high and it was out of character for Brian. In normal circumstances he was a fair man. Alf pulled off Bobby Charlton, who being the eldest player in the team was really feeling the heat; he'd already shed ten pounds since arrival. It still looked like we could hold on even though all the players were huffing and puffing, and the English nation held their breath at home. Nine minutes from the final whistle, however, Uwe Seeler, scored a back header from an acute angle and the game was taken into extra time. This was a reprise of the 1966 scenario but this time the outcome was to be different. Norman Hunter was brought on in place of Martin Peters and the flagging England team seemed to lose all its shape. The Germans advanced and the English defended but they were constantly on the back foot until finally the inevitable happened and Muller hooked one in. Pack your bags time.

We were a sad party on the flight home from Mexico. Bobby Charlton, Brian Labone, Keith Newton and Peter Bonetti would never play for England again. Other older members of the squad, like Ray Wilson, George Cohen and Roger Hunt, announced their retirement from international football.

Jack Charlton saw Alf sitting alone on the plane and sat down next to him. 'Alf, I want to thank you for giving me an international career that I thought I'd never have. I'll always be grateful for that. But Alf, I'm 35 years old now, I think it's time to give the young 'uns a turn. What I'm trying to say is I think I should retire from international football.'

'I agree,' replied Alf, barely moving his lips and looking straight ahead.

As we parted company back at Heathrow Alf looked over at me and said, 'Thanks for everything, Ossie.'

'Thanks for everything, Alf,' I said, not sure why.

The thing that cracked me up about Peter Osgood was that he would not run 5 yards for a ball, but he'd run 50 for a fight.
D. Brenan, Arsenal Supporter

9

Our Cup Runneth Over

WE WENT INTO THE 1970–71 SEASON FULL OF HOPE, ANTICIPATION HIGH. THE team was humming, we knew each other inside out – just like the Kenton Lane boys – and we were mates and would die for one another. We were proud of our on-field reputation as a fair side and an entertaining one, and were keen to prove that you didn't have to be dirty or boring to win the League. We were bullish about our chances in the European Cup-Winners' Cup but we really wanted the League Championship. The only additions to the squad were forward Keith Weller from Millwall and defender Paddy Mulligan from Shamrock Rovers. Alan Birchenall had moved on to Crystal Palace. The Selhurst Park club was soon to resemble a rehab clinic for ex-Chelsea stars; besides Birch, Bobby Tambling and Charlie Cooke both spent time there. It was sad to see Birch go. We'd all gotten attached to him and he was a great, fun bloke. He fancied himself as a crooner and would crack us all up by bursting into song at the most unlikely times in the most unlikely places – official receptions overseas, airports and during team talks to name a few.

We went six league games unbeaten, although there were a few draws in the run, before ironically losing to Leeds at Elland Road. We disposed of Aris Salonika and CSKA Sofia 6–2 and 2–0 respectively on aggregate in the first and second rounds of the Cup-Winners' Cup and kept in touch with the league leaders with pretty good results, although we were dropping more points than was desirable for a Championship-winning side. We just had to hope Arsenal and Leeds, who were blazing the trail, would hit a bad patch. Sofia, the Bulgarians, were a top side and when we had beaten them people began to think we could go all the way in Europe. Salonika were a bunch of dirtbags though. The man marking me kept touching me up and the crowd covered me and anyone else that came within coughing range in spit. I missed a penalty at their place but laid one on for Hutch. Back at the Bridge I had to come off after 20 minutes when the man with the wandering hands really gave me a dig.

Domestically the Football Association was beginning to worry about a perceived slippage in discipline among footballers. On the pitch bookings were up, and off the pitch some footballers were being accused of bringing the game into disrepute. George Best, for example, was disappearing for days on end and missing training. He had become a law unto himself. I think the FA were concerned they were losing their grip. They were. Best was summoned before them when he picked up two bookings. He got away with a fine, but I think they decided to make an example of the next naughty boy, and preferably someone whose profile was not so high as Georgie boy's. Step forward Ossie.

Ever since I had broken the leg I had become a different footballer. I looked after myself more by toughening up my act. I put out a bit more and sent out messages to defenders not to go over the top on me. If someone was aggressive, I was aggressive back. If someone tried to kick me, I'd kick them back. Sometimes I'd get my defence in first just to show them I was having none. This obviously resulted in increased interaction with the men in black. By January 1971, when Manchester City put us out in the fourth round of the FA Cup, I had picked up a third booking and I was summoned to a disciplinary hearing at Lancaster Gate. Suited and booted, Dave Sexton, Brian Mears (now chairman of the club) and myself ran the gauntlet of photographers and went inside. The smell of Werther's Originals was overwhelming. I sat there like a schoolboy caught smoking behind the science lab as these old guffers sat there and mumbled into their waistcoats. The upshot was that I was fined £150 and banned from playing football for six weeks. This was quite a punishment, and at a crucial point in our season. The three of us were left speechless and dejected. On the way home Brian Mears lifted our spirits. 'Don't worry, we will appeal,' he said defiantly. 'The FA owe a great deal to my father. We'll rattle a few cages.'

So we appealed and went through the whole charade again. They listened to our case and promptly added two weeks to my ban. Brian certainly rattled a few cages.

I knew I was being made an example of because Chelsea's reputation as hard-drinking playboys was beginning to niggle in high places, as well as causing Dave Sexton some embarrassment and annoyance. It seemed that every other week someone at the club was getting a disciplinary, or a player had been involved in some incident or other involving drink. Also the rumours started to fly about; Hudson did this, Ossie did that, Eddie Mac was . . . and so on. The facts blurred with the fiction. One of the more famous of these wild tales was that before a particular home match, by a quarter to three I was nowhere to be found, so Sexton sent Harry Medhurst over to the Rising Sun, the pub opposite the Shed End entrance, to fetch me out. Pure fantasy. I never drank in the Rising Sun.

George Thomson, a lovely director of our club, insisted on paying my fine, which was a kind gesture. He was a dear old boy and sometimes invited me to his house on St George's Hill in Weybridge to play snooker. If I thought our house in Tadworth was posh, this gaff took the biscuit! I had never seen such wealth. John Lennon lived on the estate, as did Bruce Forsyth and a host of other celebrities. It was like stepping into the pages of *Hello* except, of course, there was no *Hello* then.

The other ridiculous thing about my ban, besides the severity, was that I wasn't even allowed to the Bridge or the training ground. What was the point in that? So the training came to me. Ron Suart drove down daily and dragged me out on to Epsom Downs for cross-country running; there was no way Dave was going to let me get out of condition. I liked Ron but I didn't look forward to his knock on the door on those foggy winter's mornings. Mind you, I got the better of him sometimes when the early morning mist still hung over the Downs and he stood there waiting for me with his stop-watch. I'd wait until I was comfortably out of his range of sight and then sit down and have a rest. When the right amount of time had elapsed I'd get up, huffing and puffing, and almost fall into Ron's arms. 'That's better Os. That's the boy. You're making the effort, son.'

The ban finished in time for the second leg of the quarter-finals of the Cup-Winners' Cup tie against Club Brugge in Belgium, but Dave called me in and told me I wasn't playing. He said he thought I wasn't match fit. This was not true. Eight weeks of one-to-one sessions with Ron had got me in better condition than I had ever been. 'Dave, you're joking!' I cried.

He wasn't, but could see how genuinely upset I was and to his credit he relented and I did play. We had lost 2–0 in the first leg and knew we really had to motor in the second to ensure progression in the competition. It was a nail-biting game. Peter Houseman got the first to make it 1–2 on aggregate, but time was running out and it wasn't until five minutes from the end that I managed to score to force extra time. Tommy and I put one away each in that extra time to see us through. I was so elated that I was back and we were through that when I scored the second I carried on running, jumped the dog track and fell to my knees and saluted the human cauldron that was the Shed. In that moment the fans and I were one, united in euphoria. It was a special moment in my life.

Bring on Manchester City in the semis! Unfortunately a knee-ligament injury kept me out of both legs but the lads managed just fine without me and we won both home and away by the single goal. Our opponents in the European Cup-Winners' Cup final were to be the mighty Real Madrid, widely regarded as one of the finest sides in the world. Their heyday had been in the 1950s and '60s but they were still a force in world football. One of their biggest names in the past had been Di Stefano, a player that various journalists had very kindly compared my style of play to, which was a great compliment. The match was to be held in Athens, Greece.

Domestically, though, we had run out of juice and dropped too many points to challenge at the death for the League Championship. Still, we managed fifth in this Arsenal's League and Cup Double-winning year. Mixed form, injury and the ban had conspired to give me my worst league goal tally ever. Keith Weller was top scorer and even midfielder John Hollins managed more league goals than my paltry five. I took great comfort from the fact that the goals I was scoring were crucial ones.

It was a muggy night in Athens for the Cup-Winners' Cup final and I was not match-fit, but I was more than happy to have a shot of cortisone in the knee. Cortisone is an amazing drug that can anaesthetise localised pain, but not diminish your ability to move and play. It didn't occur to any of us that we should consider the long-term effects of these injections. It should have occurred to someone, though, because it seems beyond medical dispute now that many footballers that were given the drug have suffered severe complications in later life. I'm one of them. I'm told that cortisone temporarily kneads muscle and bone tissue together at the expense of permanently weakening the bone and tissue. Basically, it was a swap of years off the natural life of your ankle or knee in exchange for 60 or 90 minutes of football. Unfortunately we didn't know that then. This night the effects of the cortisone lasted long enough for me to score a goal that we all thought had won us our first-ever European trophy. I had to come off when the cortisone mask slipped and the pain returned, but despite some masterly play from their midfielder Pirri we hung on to the dying seconds. I even saw some officials bring out the cup in readiness, the ribbons floating in the light evening breeze. But somehow they sneaked one in and took the game to extra time. That last half-hour was uneventful and I can remember it not being frenetic like many other extra times – we were all at ease with ourselves. I, for one, felt that our name was on the cup and that destiny would take care of itself. The replay was scheduled for the coming Friday night. What was it about Chelsea, cup finals and replays?

The Greek capital had been taken over by Chelsea fans and now they were furiously ringing their mums, wives or girlfriends, and their bosses, to extend their leave. Not a lot of scaffolding was done in south and west London that week. Most had no money left, understandably budgeting for only a one or two night stay but the Greek hoteliers were unbelievable allowing, in many cases, the fans to stay on at reduced rates or even gratis. Those who couldn't get a deal made temporary accommodation on the beach. Those with money shared it with those without and bar owners displayed an almost wartime spirit of generosity. There was a marvellous atmosphere all in all and today I am still told by fans of how friendships formed in that week have endured and how a handful of Chelsea fans never came home and made Athens their permanent place to live.

The next day I fancied a drink and with Tommy and Charlie meandered up to the Hilton Hotel where we changed into our swimming gear, found a nice spot by the pool and proceeded to demolish a conveyor belt of cocktails. A few fans wandered in and out but none really invaded our privacy. That was the thing about the Chelsea fans – we never tried to be aloof from them, the opposite really, and in return they never really got in our faces.

Cocktails slide down, and when you're sitting in the sun, you don't realise how pissed you are until you try and stand up. By the time Alan Hudson arrived the three of us were rocking. He looked horrified. 'What are you doing?' he exclaimed.

'Having a drink, what do you think we are doing?' I laughed.

'But Os, we're playing tomorrow and you three are legless.'

'Don't you worry about that, young Huddy,' I assured him through glazed eyes. 'I will win the game for us tomorrow.'

Tommy and Charlie nodded in agreement.

'Now, sit down and have a nice smooth cocktail.'

That was one of the few times I saw Alan Hudson refuse a drink. He turned in disgust and walked back to our official hotel. As for us three, we kept going, finally staggering home after dark and after eight hours on the piss.

Friday came, the hangover lifted eventually, and we got out on that pitch and played a blinder. All of us. The drinkers and the abstainers. The vodka and the tonic. Tommy fired one in that the Madrid goalkeeper just managed to push over the bar. Charlie took the corner and John Dempsey, who had quietly moved forward, volleyed home. We were on the way. Then Tommy, again, laid a ball in my path. I let rip from about 25 yards and the ball just seared into the net. My goal was to prove to be the winner although I had to limp off eventually and the young South African Derek Smethurst replaced me.

Madrid came back with some spirited football in the second half, but Peter Bonetti was superb, as was Alan Hudson in the middle and we held on. Huddy had the ability to turn games around. His ability to change pace could wrong-foot anyone. Many times I had seen him collect the ball, drag it back from an advancing player, turn, look up and then go up two or three gears with a run finished off with a perfect pass into the path of Tommy or myself.

That night we went out and celebrated in a number of bars and generally bathed in the adoration of the fans. That was the loveliest thing about winning cups – seeing and joining in with the absolute delight and delirium of the supporters. They had waited a long time for the glory days to return to the Bridge. Actually, the 1955 League Championship was a bit of a one-off – *these* were the glory days. Mick Greenaway was 'Zigger Zaggering' his way through the bars of Athens that night, his nose seeming to have been squashed further into his face now, perhaps confirming the stories we were hearing about mass terrace battles between the skinhead football gangs. He and his followers were all perfect gentlemen, though, as he introduced us to various friends of his all with 'don't ask' nicknames – 'This is Jesus from the Shed and this is Psycho from the North Stand.'

'Pleased to meet you Psycho.'

We were as euphoric as they were because few of us really saw ourselves as players passing through, we were all Chelsea. True Blue as they say. We were supporters fortunate enough to be playing for the club we loved. Chelsea had that effect on players – once you arrived at Stamford Bridge, being a Chelsea player seemed to define you whether you had risen through the ranks or whether you were a signing. And as I and others found out, even when you left you were basically still a Chelsea player plying your trade elsewhere. It was the footballing equivalent of the actor's complaint of being typecast.

We flew home the next day. I remember it was hot even back in England and as we travelled up the M4 fans lined the motorway verges draping their flags and banners on the grass for us to glimpse. I wanted to get out the coach and shake each person by the hand. They were there all the way from the airport back into London. It was a fabulous sight. Everywhere people wanted to squeeze our hands and pat our backs. The world was smiling as we went to Chelsea Town Hall for the second time in a year to parade a cup around the streets of Fulham and Chelsea. The first time Webby had leant down from the open-topped bus and handed the FA Cup to a group of old Chelsea pensioners, First World War or even Boer War veterans resplendent in their red tunics and black caps. Then, as now, I just sat and smiled on that bus, secure in the loving embrace of the Chelsea family. I counted my blessings. I had come back from a broken leg, fallen in with the greatest bunch of lads you could imagine, won an FA Cup and a European Cup-Winners' Cup and played for England in Mexico. That night I went home to Tadworth to the family and fell tired but exquisitely content into my bed of roses.

Peter Osgood was a great player in an era when there was a surplus of gifted, talented footballers in the game. For me, as a midfielder, he was a joy to play with. You knew if you knocked the ball up to him he'd hold it up and do something with it. He was big and strong and very skilful – those attributes rarely go hand in hand. He was also very brave and could look after himself if need be.

I remember a game at the Bridge when I was playing for Arsenal and I scored with a header. Ossie went mad at his team mates, 'How can you let a midget score with his head', he screamed. I just ran past him laughing. When he saw me laughing he couldn't help laughing himself. That was the thing with Os he couldn't, still can't, stay serious for too long.

A. Ball, World Cup Winner

10

From a King to a Saint

IT WAS 1971–72. THE PORTENTS WERE GOOD. HUDDY WAS THE MAN OF THE moment. The papers were screaming that he should be in the England team, but Sir Alf Ramsey was not listening. They wanted Alan to model their shirts, drive their cars and drink in their clubs, yet the boy was barely 20. He engaged the fast lane like it had been built just for him. The Kings Road was his birthplace and his playground and growing up in that cosmopolitan area made him equally at home with the likes of actress Jane Seymour or photographer Terence Donovan as he would be with Maisie and Fred from the fruit and veg shop. I was a country boy really, and although Alan was my junior it was he that dragged me around the clothes shops and introduced me to the clubs of the period, such as Tramps. Much has been made of my Kings Road gallivanting, but Huddy, Tommy and Charlie were the top scoopers. They were single and lived locally, I was married with two children and lived over in Windsor. My circumstances restricted me and that was no bad thing.

As the team got bigger so did the celebrity patronage of the club. We were friendly by now with Sir Dickie Attenborough, and Michael Caine and Michael Crawford were regulars when they were in the country. There was a clique of young actors who became our mates, including Richard O'Sullivan and Robin Nedwell who were a top television draw at the time in the *Doctor in the House* programmes, a sort of *Men Behaving Badly* meets *Casualty*. Imagine my surprise when I walked into the dressing-room one Saturday after a match and I saw

Eddie Mac sitting on the bench. His glasses were perched on the end of his nose, he was puffing on a cigarette and in deep conversation with a familiar-looking man dressed smartly in a polo neck and slacks. 'Ossie, this is Steve McQueen,' he says.

And it was. Dickie Attenborough had brought him to a match and he had asked to meet the players. For once I was lost for words. I think I said something predictable like, 'I really enjoy your films.' This was true. I loved McQueen. I could watch *The Great Escape* over and over again, actually as it is on television every Christmas I do watch it over and over again. I was tongue-tied in the presence of the great man and forgot to ask for his autograph.

But I was on much better form when I met Racquel Welch. Miss Welch was massive at the time. She was pretty famous too. The apparition of her appearing from the sea dressed only in a skimpy stone-age fur bikini from the film *One Million Years BC* inspired many a young boy (and 25-year-old footballers come to that). She was over from America promoting a film, I think, and her PR people thought it a good publicity stunt if she went to a football match and where better than Stamford Bridge? They made a big thing about introducing us and she gave me a kiss on the cheek and I gave her one in return for the benefit of the assembled photographers, but unfortunately that was that. If I had been George Best I would have slipped her my number but then again if I was George Best she would have slipped me hers. I don't think she really understood football, because when she left the game had kicked off and she walked down the touchline, next to the dog track, to a cacophony of wolf-whistles and cries of 'Get 'em off!' Then the crowd joined in. She saw me, waved and shouted to get my attention, 'Wooeeee, Ossie, bye-bye Ossie.' Miss Welch probably figured, as I was standing there on the pitch doing nothing, it was okay to interrupt.

This really was our pop star period, for it was in this season that we released our first pop single as a team. I was no stranger, of course, to the world of rock, having been a key voice in the seminal *Back Home* recorded by the England/Mexico squad. The record was made, hopefully, to coincide with our victorious retention of the World Cup – that was not to be – but the song still powered to the number one spot, toppling Norman Greenbaum's 'Spirit in the Sky'. Arsenal jumped on the bandwagon, releasing 'Rule Britannia' reworked as 'Good Old Arsenal' when they won the Double, but the song only limped up the chart, peaking at number 16. The Chelsea boys did it in style, laying down 'Blue is the Colour', a song written especially for us by Peter Lee Stirling and Daniel Boone. It was catchy and original, and for a football team song it was a different class. It went to number five, being outsold most noticeably by T Rex's 'Telegram Sam' and Chicory Tip's 'Son of My Father', but in those days to reach that position you had to sell around half a million copies. Either Chelsea's extended fan base was larger than Arsenal's and bigger than most imagined, or the song had crossed over into the mainstream big style. We even did *Top of the Pops* with that amiable crank, Jimmy Savile. The record company were so confident about us that day in the studio we laid down an album of covers and I sang lead vocals on a now legendary version of 'Chirpy Chirpy Cheep Cheep', first recorded by Middle of the Road. If you thought the original was bad (it is one of those records that no one admits to buying, yet curiously it held the number one spot for five weeks in 1971) you should hear mine. Surely you haven't forgotten those lyrics, tinged with sorrow? Inexplicably, the album flopped.

It was in this period that I met a successful businessman named Ray Bloye. He ran a butchery business from offices in Epsom and had the full millionaire's lifestyle. He really wanted to get on the board at Chelsea and probably had designs to take it over should the opportunity arise. Maybe he thought I could open doors for him but Mears and the boys were pretty much a closed shop in those days. We became friendly and he loaned me his brown 4.2 XJ6 Jaguar motor. As if lending me the car was not enough he pointed me towards his personal fuel account at a garage in Wimbledon and I filled up whenever I wanted. Not only did he provide me with a luxury car and free petrol, he gave me a set of keys to his luxury Dolphin Square apartment. His wife suffered from Alzheimer's, or senile decay as they called it then, and she lived next door in an adjoining flat with round-the-clock nursing. This was the life. Cruising down the Kings Road to pick up Huddy, Tommy, Charlie or Eddie – whoever was up for it and then on to a club to pull some birds and if we were lucky back to the pad in Dolphin Square to round off the night. Now and then he even loaned me his blue Rolls Royce, and I'm sure that when us boys pulled up outside the Markham, the Trafalgar or the Chelsea Potter on the Kings Road, the locals must have shook their heads and thought, 'These modern footballers really are getting paid too much.'

We were safe on the Kings Road and around Fulham. We could waltz around, let our hair down and be off our guard because people rarely had a pop even though we were famous. The Chelsea people closed ranks around us. Only a tiny fraction of our escapades made it back to Dave Sexton (although he wasn't stupid and was well aware of the situation), and more importantly to the press. The Kings Road community looked after us and gave us plenty of safe houses. One such place was Alexandres, a Fulham restaurant run by two delightful gay fellas, Camillo and Manuel. All sorts, from visiting Wimbledon tennis players such as Jimmy Connors and Chris Evert, to politicians and film stars used it but it was most famous for being the place the Chelsea players hung out. It would be unusual to go in there and not see one of the squad, whether it be Webby tucking into steak and red wine or Eddie perched on a stool at the bar sipping brandy. Only on Saturday afternoons would you be hard pushed to find one of us.

Celebrating after our victory against Spurs which secured our place in the League Cup final, we spilled out of Alexandres, me, Chrissy Garland, Huddy and Danny Gillen, a pal of his. Alan was on a particular high because he had scored a marvellous goal straight from a corner kick. We were pleasantly but not wildly drunk, and singing, which drew some attention as it was by now the early hours of the morning. Someone complained and before we knew it we were surrounded by police. For some reason, I cannot fathom why, they were up for a row. They started to manhandle us although we were offering no resistance whatsoever. 'Get in your car and piss off home, Osgood,' one officer growled at me.

'Yeah, so you can nick him,' interjected Danny Gillen.

The officer shoved Danny. He was a big guy and he turned around and knocked the policeman clean out. All hell was let loose and I was bundled into a Black Maria. I was sobering up fast.

Back at the station I was charged with being drunk and disorderly, put in a cell and a couple of hours later given my car keys and sent off home. A few weeks later I was up at Marylebone Magistrates Court and couldn't believe my ears when I heard the account given by the police. I had been singing, according to them, not 'Chirpy Chirpy Cheep Cheep' but anti-Semitic football songs, I was so drunk I could barely stand and I resisted arrest by swearing and shoving.

'The defendant was extremely drunk, in your opinion, officer?' quizzed the magistrate.

'Oh yes, sir. He was very, very drunk.'

'So why did you hand a very, very drunken man his car keys and send him on his way just one hour and forty-seven minutes after his arrest?'

I was found not guilty.

After 18 months of my using the Jag, Ray Bloye suggested I bought it from him.

'How much?' I asked.

'Two thousand five hundred,' he replied. I thought about it but concluded what with my new mortgage I couldn't really afford it.

'Fair enough,' said Mr Bloye, 'come and see me in Epsom on Monday.'

I turned up at his offices fully expecting to return the keys and the car. I had had a good run. Instead he handed me a brown envelope.

'What's this?' I enquired.

'Two thousand five hundred pounds to pay for the car. Just hand it back to me and the car is yours.'

It was bizarre, but he said something about keeping his company books straight and I kept the car. I did lay off his personal petrol account though!

Shortly after I guess he realised that far from opening doors to the Chelsea high and mighty I was probably closing them, and he turned his attentions to Crystal Palace. He bought the struggling First Division side and under him they enjoyed some of their most memorable years as he installed Malcolm Allison as manager and attracted great players such as Don Rogers and Peter Taylor.

Cars generally were beginning to cause me problems. On the way home one night I was pulled up by the police and asked to blow in the dreaded bag, and not surprisingly I was asked to appear at court. Two weeks later, before my court appearance, I was flagged down again near Heathrow Airport on the way back from visiting Eddie McCreadie. I had only had a couple of pints and was really quite angry at what I then saw as harassment.

'What colour is the car you are driving?' was the policeman's second question after enquiring as to whether I had been drinking. What sort of a question is that?

'Fucking pink,' I retorted.

They bundled me into their car and drove me to Staines police station, with another policeman following behind in my car. The arresting officer was pleased as punch with himself when he booked me in at the desk. He was like an angler landing a lovely big fish. The sergeant on the desk, noting that my earlier reading had been borderline, said that I should have the opportunity to blow in the bag again. I thought this was decent of him. Again the result was borderline. The first policeman argued in front of me that it was over the limit.

'Not in my eyes it's not,' said the sergeant. 'Mr Osgood, take your keys and drive carefully.'

'Thanks officer,' I smiled.

'Sergeant,' he corrected me, as the traffic policeman looked on, his face frozen with anger. As he held the back door open for me to the station car park he winked and whispered, 'Blue is the colour.'

Fortunately or unfortunately, depending on how you look at it, the magistrate at Kingston Court was not a Chelsea fan. A few weeks later he banned me from driving for a year.

We had signed Chrissy Garland from Bristol City in the close season. A striker, he was a good-looking blond kid who looked like he'd be more at home on Bondi beach with a surfboard under his arm than the west country of England. He became one of the chaps from the day he turned up. He was a nifty goal-getter on the field and as mad as a hatter off it. He fitted in well. One time he was giving me a lift in my car when his erratic driving attracted the attentions of a police officer, who flagged us down. He started taking Chris's details whilst radioing through for confirmation of ownership. He rested his pen, notebook and some papers on the roof of the car. To my horror Chris switched on the ignition, started the car and roared off. Out of the driver's mirror I could see the papers flapping in the road and the officer waving at us forlornly. It was like a scene from a Will Hay film.

Steve Kember came from Crystal Palace, where he was top jolly although still only 22 years of age. Steve was a midfielder and his signing unsettled Huddy and Charlie a bit. Keith Weller, who had played such a crucial part in the Cup-Winners' Cup success, slipped off quietly to Leicester City. I'm surprised Stevie joined us, for not long before Chopper had given him the famous elbow in the mouth and knocked his front teeth out. Not long after he arrived we were playing Leeds and I was about to do the very same thing to Johnny Giles, who was really asking for it this day, but as my elbow came crashing down I saw Johnny's head move and the innocent elfin features of Stevie take the full impact. This time he was spitting out his new set of teeth.

It was not a great season but not a disastrous one either. It opened at Highbury, where Arsenal displayed their two trophies, and we chucked in our European Cup for the crowd, but the Double-winners caned us 3–0. We were put out of the Cup-Winners' Cup by Atvidaberg of Sweden, losing on the away goal, and shockingly got dumped out of the FA Cup by lowly Orient in the fifth round. The Chelsea fans invaded the pitch here in a failed effort to get the match stopped and avoid the humiliation. We ended a respectable seventh in the league and I was the club's top scorer with 18 goals. This was the year that Brian Clough's Derby County side nipped in and took the league from under the noses of Don Revie's Leeds United. That cheered us up a little. Poor old Hutch had been out all season. Injuries were to ruin his career, the penalty he paid for being the bravest man ever to pull on a Chelsea shirt.

Dear Hutch. He was always in the wars. He hadn't been with us long when I noticed that he seemed very worried in the changing-room before a game with Nottingham Forest up at their place.

'What's up Hutch?' I asked.

'There's a geezer playing today who I know,' he explained. He's a hard bastard and when I played for Burton Albion he used to really come out to hurt me. He doesn't like me, Os.'

I would never have thought that Hutch was scared of anyone, but this defender had obviously hurt him as a young player and it had affected him.

'Hutch, you play for Chelsea, you're a star now. He's a nobody.'

'That's what I'm worried about,' said Hutch as he gathered himself and walked out on the pitch deep in thought.

Ten minutes in I glanced at him and noticed his eye was swollen. Hutch pointed at his elbow and then nodded over at the Forest bully, indicating he had whacked him. Just before the half-time whistle Hutch jumped for a ball and then clattered to the ground clutching his face, claret seeping through his fingers. The thug had done him again with his elbow, the footballer's weapon of choice. In the dressing-room he could barely speak as he examined the damage to his nose. We would find out later that it was actually broken but Hutch insisted on playing on. By now I was fuming.

'Listen up Hutch. When we get out there as soon as we get a corner, we'll get Charlie to chip the ball near the post. I'll fall on Grummit and generally cause a little row to distract the ref and you'll be behind. Turn round and whack bollock-face as hard as you can. Knock the bastard out.'

For the first time that afternoon a smile broke out across Hutch's face. Sure enough, we got a corner within ten minutes and Charlie chipped the ball exactly where I had told him. I smacked poor Peter Grummit, their goalie, as hard as I could with my shoulder and fell on to him. As we tussled, the referee came running over blowing his whistle loudly. I heard the thump and thought, 'Well done big fella.' When I emerged from my scrum Hutch's tormentor was looking down scowling at Ian. He was on the floor clutching his forearm and screaming, 'I've broke my arm Os.' He had.

At the start of the season Dave Sexton had very publicly slammed my performance against Manchester United when we lost 3–2 at the Bridge and he transfer-listed me. This shocked me and seemed like a disproportionate reaction to a poor performance. Looking back I wonder if Dave was looking for an excuse to get me out of the club even then. Then, just like when Tommy had transfer-listed Barry Bridges all those years before, there was an outcry. The fans organised demonstrations and petitions and Dave took me off the list. I also heard that Bill Shankly came in for me, but flattering as it was I don't know if I could ever have seriously contemplated a career up north.

Ironically I really loved my football at this time. I had a great rapport with the crowd, not only at Chelsea but across the whole country. I did come in for stick but most of the time it seemed good-natured. English football crowds love flair players, whoever they are, and can be extraordinarily generous to footballers from opposing sides if they entertain them. In one game, I think it was Leicester, I wasn't getting much of the ball so I wandered over to the wing and sat on the wall separating the crowd from the pitch, crossed my arms and had a chat with the spectators. I always made a point of acknowledging the Shed, especially when they lauded me with the 'Born is the King of Stamford Bridge' song. Having 50,000 people sing about you in that way is the most marvellous feeling. I wish I had savoured the occasions more, but I guess I thought they would never end.

We did make Wembley again that season, even if it was in the less illustrious League Cup final. We beat arch-enemies Spurs in the two-legged semi-final 5–4 on aggregate. Chris Garland was on good form, scoring two of the goals and me, Huddy and Johnny Hollins got the other three. In between the two semis we played Ipswich at the Bridge. It was 27 December and the pitch was a mud bath. The game sticks in my mind because due to an unforeseen chain of events concerning our goalkeepers, David Webb played in goal. Peter Bonetti, being a family man, was usually not around at Christmas and John Phillips couldn't be contacted. Our third-choice keeper Steve Sherwood dropped everything to get to the game, but public transport being what it is, he didn't make it in time.

At the beginning of the game Webby dropped to his knees in the goalmouth, placed his palms together and feigned praying. It was a very funny moment, but he need not have worried as we won 2–0 and Dave holds a 100 per cent clean sheet as a goalkeeper. Another time, when the pitch was a mud bath, he launched himself forward to head a ball and ended sliding along the ground head first in a mud track. Instead of jumping to his feet, he lay there and simulated swimming. These fun moments were caught on camera and along with Terry Venables and his wiggling eyebrows were among the more memorable clips regularly replayed on ITV's *The Big Match* on a Sunday afternoon.

It was against Ipswich that Alan Hudson scored the goal that never was. His shot thumped into the side netting but the referee, who must have used the same optician as Ronnie and Eddie, blew for a goal. The Ipswich players went berserk and pleaded with Alan to tell the referee but contrary to popular belief, Huddy did not and ran back into his half to take up his position. The goal stood.

We were expected to win the League Cup final against Stoke. They were bobbing around the lower reaches of the First Division and were generally considered to be an old man's side. Gordon Banks was still in goal and up front were Peter Dobing and, wait for it, George Eastham – the very man who had stared down at me from my bedroom wall when I was a kid. What sheltered housing they sprung him from I'll never know. I didn't know he was still alive, let alone still playing! Stoke's striker Terry Conroy scored early with a header and this shook us to the core, but close to half-time I managed to equalise from a shot as I stumbled down onto one knee. In the second half we dominated the match and I felt it would only be a matter of time before we prevailed. Chris Garland had come close to scoring a few times, but against the run of play George Eastham seized on the ball as it ran loose after Peter Bonetti had saved from Jimmy Greenhoff and tucked it away. It was a lesson in irony for me. A man from the pages of *Football Monthly* and days of brown leather footballs with laces, who I had watched as a kid at Highbury and thought had long ago hung up his boots, breezed back into my life in the dying embers of his career with deadly effect. The day belonged to Gentleman George and the men from the Potteries. It was their first honour in over a century.

I suppose you could carbon date the start of Chelsea Football Club's and my own footballing decline from that day and George's goal. Events conspired to change all of our lives. The failure to win a trophy upset Dave Sexton and his willingness to turn a blind eye to our social life ended. A police car chase involving Tommy Baldwin in which a vodka bottle was thrown from a car window seemed to encapsulate how wild we had become. Luckily the bottle didn't hit Tommy. Brian Mears had embarked on a reconstruction of the Chelsea ground, which was running behind time and massively over budget. Whispers of a financial squeeze at the club hung in the air. Football hooligans had come to prominence and in keeping with the image, the ones from Chelsea made more headlines than most.

On a footballing level Huddy was becoming disillusioned. Dave had moved him out onto the flank to accommodate Steve Kember. He couldn't see the point of that – it wasn't as if he wasn't delivering in his midfield role – and he didn't like it out there. It must have felt as though he was being deliberately handicapped.

Eddie McCreadie ran into some real personal problems at this time. He was feeling the pressure to perform more than the rest of us and he disliked the whole fame thing. He entered what I recognise now as a depressive state. At the time it was like, 'snap out of it Eddie'. But when he made an attempt at cutting his wrists we knew he was in a bad way. We went to where he was living when he was really poorly and his eyes were far away. I sat up with him to the early hours of the morning drinking brandy and milk. He sat cross-legged on the floor and just rocked backward and forward. Another time Webby was there with me and we both just looked at one another, really scared. This was out of our league. Things like this were not meant to happen to football players. Eddie eventually had to spend some time in a psychiatric hospital before he was right again, but the breakdown, because that's what it was, really scarred him.

We all worried about Hutch. Two broken legs and a host of other injuries had rendered him very vulnerable and we felt responsible because most of his injuries were picked up looking out for us. Charlie, too, was becoming a bit introspective and Webby did not like the way that Dave was tinkering with the team and breaking it up unnecessarily. He was particularly unhappy I recall when he offloaded Keith Weller.

114

Tommy Baldwin was sick of not always being an automatic first team choice. We were all still drinking, but slowly but surely it seemed that we had stopped chasing the buzz and were drinking to wipe away the nagging pain of a party coming to an end. Bill Garner's arrival from the lower leagues did little to give Hutch or Tommy any comfort. Bill had impressed Dave in a match against Southend United. He was a big fearless lad who had a temper on him. First Division defenders soon learned not to cross him. So did we. In a match against Liverpool he scraped Emlyn Hughes' shin leaving a cut that required stitches. 'That's for Ossie,' he told him. I don't ever remember telling Bill about the Hughes business, it certainly wasn't playing on my mind. He was like a pit-bull terrier straining at the leash.

The season 1972–73 was Chelsea's worst campaign for a number of years. No Europe. We went out in the League Cup to Norwich City in the semi-finals round and Arsenal beat us in the quarter-finals of the FA Cup, although it was close and we took them to a replay. In the league, we slipped to 12th position, our lowest placing in a decade. I got 17 goals overall, 11 only in the League. Chris Garland tied with me as top scorer.

Dave Sexton was really on my case. I think he saw Huddy and me as the ringleaders of the naughty-boy culture. He may have been right. I think he resented us too because we *could* do the things we did. By all accounts Dave was a good player, but not a great one, and he really had to work at his game to attain the level he did. I think he found it frustrating that us two had the talent and didn't treasure and nurture it in the way he would have.

His attitude to me in training shifted significantly. One day he bellowed at me, 'Ten press-ups Ossie.'

I ignored him at first but he roared again. I stood there, hands on my hips, and just looked at him. This wasn't a short, sharp shock institution after all. The rest of the players stopped as Dave steamed over and shoved me. 'Don't push me, Dave,' I warned, but Dave in full flow was a frightening prospect. His dad Archie had been a professional boxer and had appeared in the first-ever televised boxing match in 1933 when he fought Laurie Raiteri in a middleweight bout. Dave was as solid as a rock and had clearly inherited the pugilistic family gene. I could see this meant a lot to him. A bit of a Terry Venables/Tommy Docherty scenario had developed very suddenly here, although it was potentially more physical.

Reading my mind, he offered me out. 'Come on then, Ossie, if you want to try it.'

The veins in his bull neck were taut like wire and his fists were clenched. I dropped to the floor and did 20 press-ups.

The following season, 1973–74, we got off to an appalling start. We lost the first 3 matches and only won 12 all season, but I was not to see out the campaign. On a personal level, I thought Dave and I were getting on better and the incident in training where I had publicly bowed down to his authority had been a watershed in our relationship. Around Christmas of 1973 he had called me into his office and asked me if I would like to take over the captaincy of the club. He said the team needed to be changed radically and this was one of the measures he was contemplating. The skipper job had been taken away from Ron Harris, passed to Eddie McCreadie and was currently being filled by John Hollins. I wasn't sure it was a good idea. 'But the players all look up to you,' Dave argued. I said I'd think about it.

I had been struggling to notch up my 100th league goal for Chelsea. I seemed to be stuck on 98 for weeks and the tension was rising with each game. They kept going on about it in the programme and it became a disproportionate worry in my mind. Finally against Everton in November 1973 I got my ton and one extra in our 3–1 victory at Stamford Bridge. The lads made a real fuss of me, as they knew the relief I was feeling.

Dave called me into his office after our home defeat against the champions, Liverpool, incorporating the young, dynamic Kevin Keegan. It was no shame to lose to Liverpool by a single goal. They were rapidly becoming the best side in Europe. I fully expected then that we were going to explore the captaincy conversation further. Instead Dave told me he wasn't happy with my form and that he was dropping me from the team for the next game against Sheffield United. I did not know then that he had had the same conversation with Alan Hudson. I also did not know that I had just played my last senior game for Chelsea for some years.

My form couldn't have been as bad as Dave implied; at least Alf Ramsey didn't think so, because he called me up for the crucial World Cup qualifier against Poland. I was surprised at my selection after three and a half years in the international wilderness. It had really come out the blue but it couldn't have been at a better time for me. The word was that Alf was frustrated with his first choice, centre-forward Martin Chivers of Spurs. It was a crucial game because England had lost to Poland in Chorzow and only drawn with the Welsh, meaning that to be sure of qualification to the 1974 World Cup finals England had to beat the Poles. Fate again took a hand and I picked up a knee injury and was unable to play. Chivers kept his place but England could only manage a 1–1 draw and the antics of the Polish keeper Tomaszewki, who grasped more balls than an army doctor that night, was the only memorable thing about the action.

The humiliation of non-qualification for the World Cup finals, won only eight short years before, was immense. Press and public reaction was vitriolic and Martin Chivers, for one, was never capped again. A few weeks later in November Alf gave me another chance. I now felt after all the stops and starts he really was going to run with me. The match was against Italy at Wembley and again England lost. Peter Shilton had by now, after waiting patiently for years, inherited England's goalkeeping mantle from Gordon Banks, but this night he dropped the ball at Chinaglia's feet and the Italian didn't miss. Good night nurse. There were three losers that night – England, Sir Alf Ramsey, who was sacked, and Peter Osgood. I never pulled on an England shirt again.

It had been Bobby Moore's last cap too and he knew it. When I had arrived at Hendon Hall, Sir Alf asked me, 'Do you mind rooming with Robert?' He meant Mooro. When I got up to the room, Bobby was standing in front of the mirror splashing the aftershave on.

'Come on Ossie, get your gladrags on. Me, you and Clarkey are going out on the piss.'

'Bob, I've waited four years for this. I am not risking anything tonight,' I protested.

'Ossie, this is my last game for England. We're going to drink to it.'

'How do you know that?'

'I just know.'

Allan Clarke arrived at the door. I couldn't disobey the captain, could I?

I knew my England career was finally over, although one could argue it had never really begun, when Alf's successor was named (following a brief caretaker interlude courtesy of Joe Mercer) – Don Revie. Upon his appointment Revie, the former Leeds manager, had said, 'One of the few successes in the side was Osgood.' But I knew it was a wind-up. Revie hated Chelsea and me especially. You think you can hear the crushing of sour grapes, I know, but it is true. The animosity between Leeds United and Chelsea was well known, we took real pleasure in beating them and vice versa. We stood for everything Revie didn't like in football, as they did for everything we didn't like. The players hated each other and so did the fans. Leeds United never forgave us for beating them in the FA Cup, and if that sounds far-fetched cast your mind back to Jack Charlton's tantrum at the end of the match. If you have laughed in a man's face when you have scored against his side and seen the suppressed anger, you know that if he could he would get even. I never really imagined that Don Revie would get the opportunity, but he did. That's life.

Without me and Huddy, with Peter Bonetti also dropped and Ronnie back as captain again, Chelsea beat Sheffield United at Bramall Lane. The team was changing shape, with newcomers Gary Locke, Mickey Droy and Ian Britton all playing that day and acquitting themselves well. Perhaps the result gave Dave the reassurance that a future without us two, the terrible twins, was one in which the team could recover and flourish. We were in the reserves now and at training that's who we played with. Dario Gradi was the reserve team manager. I didn't take to Dario – he was always a bit aloof and gave off the vibe that he was a bit special in football when in fact I didn't think he was. Unless playing for Sutton United in the Southern League and running a blow football shop in Ewell Village makes you special. He's done great things in his time at Crewe Alexandra, but remember this was long, long before he became manager up there. My dislike for him stemmed from an earlier incident, when I played against Reading in the reserves while coming back from injury. Something popped in my groin and I came off. Gradi thought I was trying it on and sneered at me: 'Thanks a lot for letting the club down.' A couple of days later I was in physio with Harry Medhurst and my groin area was black and blue where a blood vessel had burst. I saw Dario and called him in. 'Take a look at that Dario. Still think I'm skiving?'

He glanced over, shrugged and walked out of the room. An apology would have been nice.

Dario said to me on this fateful day, 'Dave wants you over there on the first team practice pitch.'

'If I'm playing for the reserves, then I'll train with the reserves,' I countered. Huddy came up behind me and said the same counted for him. Gradi shot off to tell the boss. Dave came over red with rage. Gradi bobbed around behind him.

'If you don't like it, you two, you can fuck off home.'

'Fine,' we said and we walked away.

'By the way,' shouted Huddy over his shoulder, 'can you get me a transfer please, Dave?'

'Yes I will, son,' he says and I'm sure he almost broke into a smile.

Bill Garner drove me and Huddy away. Literally an hour or two later we picked up a copy of the *Evening Standard*, only to see the back-page headline screaming 'OSGOOD AND HUDSON DEMAND TRANSFER'. Someone at the club had wasted little time in ensuring that the no-turning-back point had been reached. Dave always maintained that I requested a transfer. That Huddy was speaking for us both. This was quite important because it meant that if I asked for a transfer it disqualified me from the 5 per cent of the transfer fee I would have been entitled to if I had been transferred at the behest of the club. And everyone knew that we were both on the transfer list because that is what Dave wanted. That stuck in my craw.

Tony Waddington, manager of the Stoke City side that had defeated us in the League Cup final, came in for Alan Hudson very quickly. £240,000 saw him drive away from the bright lights of Chelsea to the industrial Potteries. Huddy was stubborn and would not have looked over his shoulder as he left, even though Stamford Bridge was his physical and spiritual home whether he admitted it or not. His stubbornness was to stand him in good stead some 25 years later when he refused point blank to die after being smashed to smithereens in a car accident.

Dave Mackay, now in Brian Clough's seat at Derby County, offered me a six-year contract but much as I admired Dave as a player and a manager, I didn't want to jump at the first offer. I still had an aversion to uprooting my family to the north of England. Jimmy Bloomfield at Leicester also made a serious enquiry, but other than that managers waving chequebooks were not battering the door down.

This was not a good time to have uncertainty around your employment. The miners had been on strike, with the ensuing power cuts affecting everyone, the country had been on a three-day week and the British people kicked out Edward Heath as Prime Minister and reinstalled Harold Wilson. The only Mr Blair around then was Lionel. The cold winds of harsh economic reality were even blowing around the football grounds of the country. Chelsea, as we know, had its own special set of financial problems. I was getting cold feet and genuinely did not want to leave the club that had been my only home for the uncertainty of another. I tried to reconcile with Dave. He seemed agreeable and said that he would speak to the chairman about renewing my contract. I breathed a sigh of relief. But when I spoke to Brian Mears some time later, he told me that Dave had not spoken to him. It was then I had to face facts. As I have said before, I am not one to get myself into a state over things that are not in your power to change. Sexton wanted me out – maybe Mears did too.

Huddy was going great guns up at Stoke. With him on board they started to motor up the table. He was probably playing the best football of his career. They even did the Double over Chelsea, with Alan having the mixed pleasure of scoring the only goal in a 1–0 win at Stamford Bridge. Geoff Hurst was also there; in fact Tony Waddington had Alan living with Geoff and his wife Judith in the hope that the domestic bliss might encourage Alan to lead a more sedentary lifestyle. No chance. 'Get up here,' advised Huddy and I opened up talks with Tony Waddington. I went as far as shaking hands with the manager after agreeing terms, but did have the proviso of telling him that I had promised to meet with Lawrie McMenemy of Southampton the next day but regarded it as a polite formality. I had come to terms with moving up to Stoke, I could play with Huddy again and we'd be able to return to our social whirl. I convinced myself it would be fun and rewarding, and if I fancied the quiet life I could always go round Geoff's.

That period when I finally left Chelsea has become shrouded in the mists of time. I heard that Brian Mears initially sacked Dave when the thing with Huddy and me came to a head, but he was obviously quickly reinstated if that were true. Dickie Attenborough told Mears not to let me and Huddy go, I am told, but Sexton said it was us or him and Brian decided to stand by the manager. I also heard that some of the lads were glad to see the back of us, which upset me although none of them said anything to me directly. I was really saddened by that, if it were the case, because I do not think I was a troublemaker. A tearaway maybe, but I knew my place and on the whole always did as I was told. I still think it is sad that things ended up as they did. We were still a relatively young team and I believe it was broken up too early. I think we could have ridden out the bad run and gone on to bigger and better things.

Lawrie McMenemy is a persuasive man, as I was to find out when I arrived at his home in Chandlers Ford near Southampton. He welcomed me at the door, let me in and then shut the door behind him. I was surprised to see him locking it. 'You are not leaving this house, Peter Osgood, until you sign for Southampton.'

I miss him.
B. Willis, Chelsea Publican

11

When the Saints

SOUTHAMPTON FOOTBALL CLUB IS A RELATIVE NEWCOMER TO THE FOOTBALL League, having entered the old Third Division South in 1920. Yet as a non-league club they had been beaten in two FA Cup finals in 1900 and 1902, so they were not without pedigree. Like Chelsea, they didn't really start to make waves until the mid-1950s, when Ted Bates became their manager. Progress under Bates was steady but sure. He quietly set about developing the side and in the 1959–60 season they won the Third Division. A couple of seasons later, as a Second Division side, they lost 1–0 to Manchester United in the FA Cup semi-final and in the 1965–66 season won promotion to the First Division for the first time.

Their first few seasons in the top flight were unremarkable, although the club did manage to avoid relegation, but in 1968–69 they finished seventh and qualified for the old Fairs Cup. It had taken 15 years but Ted Bates, a real old-school manager and gentleman, had taken the Saints from the Third Division to European football. I know from direct experience that the team of that period played entertaining football; matches against Southampton always seemed to produce goals. Big John McGrath shored up the defence in that side, Terry Paine, an all-time hero at the Dell and an England international, was still there but it was the strike force of young Mick Channon and Welsh centre-forward Ron Davies that really powered them forward. Davies was lethal with his head and for some years when the top goalscorers of the season were listed, Ron, you could be sure, was there or thereabouts. The following season they found themselves back scrapping away with the relegation candidates, but in 1970–71 they climbed back to seventh place and qualified this time for the UEFA Cup. In 1971–72 they were back down at 19th place, but in 1972–73 they hauled themselves back up to 12th. During the 1973–74 season Ted Bates, who had transformed the club and completed an unthinkable (these days) nearly 20 years as manager, stepped aside for a tall former guardsman with a Geordie accent.

Lawrie McMenemy had been a professional footballer in the lower leagues, most notably for former league club Gateshead, but like a number of successful managers had never really made the big time as a player. He made a name for himself as a young, thrusting manager with Doncaster Rovers and then Grimsby Town, taking Grimsby out of the Fourth Division as champions in the 1971–72 season. When he took the job at the Dell, the Saints were sitting at fifth in the First Division but by the time of our meeting in March 1974 the season was drawing to a close and the team had repeated their usual yo-yo pattern and fallen down into the relegation zone. I was not too concerned, as the Saints had formed a habit of successfully avoiding the drop for nearly a decade now.

I was impressed with what he had to tell me. He was looking at the long-term future of the club. Not interested in short-term fixes. He had no doubt that within two or three seasons the Saints would be challenging for, and winning, major honours. He pointed to the club's catchment area and the potential for big crowds. He told me about his personal ambitions – how he would revolutionise the club from top to bottom. Importantly, he said he would not try and change me, that he believed flair and skill should be nourished and not blunted.

This was all music to my ears at a time when I was feeling disillusioned and unappreciated. It is no accident that these days Lawrie trains professional business managers in motivational skills. Suddenly I was not a playboy footballer with ever-decreasing options, but the foundation block in a talented young manager's vision to create a new force in football. I was 27 years old and could picture myself playing down there until I was 32 or 33, putting Southampton on the map and then, who knows, maybe moving into coaching or management with Lawrie and the dynamic set-up he would surely build.

I felt bad about letting Tony Waddington at Stoke down. He too was a smashing bloke, but I felt that he'd been at Stoke a long time. He had taken over in 1960 when Stanley Matthews was still playing and although he had signed Huddy, the club had a reputation for being a place where old 'names' went out to grass – George Eastham, Peter Dobing, David Herd and Geoff Hurst to name but a few. More importantly, Southampton was down south and Stoke was very much up north. Us Osgoods have never been adventurous in the geographical sense. Finally, Lawrie was willing to do a deal where Southampton Football Club would make a donation to my testimonial fund, which would go some way to compensating me for the five per cent of the £275,000 transfer fee I felt was due to me. Like the old TV advert where a bank manager appears out of a cupboard, Lawrie brought some legal people into the room and I signed for Southampton Football Club there and then.

The lads made me feel welcome immediately. Hughie Fisher, Jim Steele, Bobby Stokes, Terry Paine, Mick Channon and the others struck me as a well-adjusted, down to earth and friendly bunch. I felt comfortable from day one. But the culture shock was immense. When I turned up for my first game and went into the changing-room I could not help but notice the most foul smell. There was no doubt it was shit, but I did not want to offend anyone so kept quiet. In the end, though, I had to say something because it was turning my stomach. 'Can anyone smell anything?' I enquired innocently. The boys all started laughing and explained that Channon and Brian O'Neill kept horses and the last thing they did before turning up for matches was muck them out.

At Chelsea, when we went to away games I was accustomed to first-class coach, rail and even air travel, and we always dressed smartly in suits or club blazers. Here they all met outside the WH Smith stand on the railway station and dressed in jeans and old T-shirts. 'Where's your overnight gear, Mick?' I asked Channon the first time. He produced a toothbrush from the pocket of his denim jacket. I had gone from playing for the country's most fashionable team to joining the Young Farmers in Football Society. I didn't know whether to laugh or cry!

One of my early games was against Chelsea. I got a mixed reception. Most of the crowd gave me an ovation, which was nice, but it hurt that there was also booing. Some parts of the crowd even chanted, 'What a waste of money.' Obviously they did not know the full story – that I did not leave Chelsea, but Chelsea left me. To them I was probably the star who got too big for his boots and bailed out when the going got tough, the star who wouldn't take the discipline. Basically in those early days I think Chelsea supporters had mixed feelings over the whole sorry business. Some were angry with the club for letting me and Huddy go and suspected that the mounting financial problems were the true motive. Others were angry at Huddy and me. That game finished in a goalless draw – a relief for me, as I didn't fancy scoring against my old club so soon after I had left and whilst the wounds were still very much open and festering. The side Chelsea fielded that day was already quite different to the one I had played with only weeks before. Ray Wilkins, a hard-running teenager, was playing only his second senior match and Kenny Swain, John Sparrow and big Mickey Droy had taken over in defence.

Rose and I sold the house in Tadworth with some regret, as we had had happy times there and the kids had been given a very good schooling. We moved to St Leonards in Windsor and purchased a lovely place for £39,000, which was better positioned motorway-wise for getting to and from my new club. Remember, the M25 was merely a twinkle in some transport planner's eye in 1974. We soon discovered that one of our new neighbours was the madcap comedian Freddie Starr, who had recently burst to national fame through an outrageous (for the time) performance in the Royal Variety Show. Although I don't think he had the slightest interest in football, we became friends and knocked around for a bit. Freddie didn't drink, thank God, because he was a maniac without it and I imagine that alcohol would have tipped him over the edge even then. His manic energy was hard to keep up with. Freddie had a little petrol motorbike, which he seemed to prefer to his white Roller, and would scramble around the drive and nearby fields. He took to riding it around my house early on a Sunday morning and then knocking at the door and, like a kid, calling up at the window: 'Rose, is Ossie coming out?'

'Tell him I'm out, tell him I'm out,' I'd hiss from beneath the covers.

As the 1973–74 season came to a close the unthinkable (for me at least) happened. Southampton and Chelsea were battling it out with Birmingham City, West Ham and Coventry to avoid relegation. It was the end of an era anyway, because Manchester United had finally bowed to the inevitable and joined Norwich City in the Second Division, but this year, for the first time, the rules had been changed and three clubs instead of two would be relegated. It was a poignant time for United and everyone who loved them, because the careers of Bobby Charlton and George Best had come to an end. Denis Law had travelled across town to Manchester City and scored the goal that had sentenced his beloved club to relegation. To cap it all, Tommy Docherty was the manager and I knew he was facing a thankless task when he took over because someone had to break up a side that had become such an institution that people refused to believe the ageing process applied to them.

It went to the wire. Chelsea managed in the end to garner 37 points and Southampton 36. Dave Sexton was under real pressure but I took no pleasure from this, I was more concerned with my own plight. I hadn't considered that Lawrie's long-term vision included relegation into the Second Division in the short term. Chelsea were floundering and I was now a Second Division footballer for the first time in my life. Life can change so radically in the space of a few months. The only winner in all of this appeared to be Alan Hudson. He had performed miracles at Stoke City. His form was scintillating – if the season could have been extended they would have won the League. In any case, from the lower reaches when he joined, Stoke City finished in a remarkable fifth place, their highest league position for 30 years. Huddy was already being lauded as the new Stanley Matthews. They loved him.

I played out the 1974–75 season at Southampton in the Second Division and we finished 13th. I really noticed the drop in class and was not very happy most of the time, I was often alone up front and without a Hutch or a Baldwin to play off I felt deserted. Despite this I did manage to score goals, but not as many as I would have liked. Lawrie was busy signing players like Ian Turner, David Peach and Peter Rodrigues, and the prospects for next season were looking better. Rodrigues was a masterstroke; a tenacious, attacking Welsh full-back, he had played for Leicester in the 1969 FA Cup final when they lost to Manchester City. He was now in the autumn of his career but, inspired by Lawrie, he in turn inspired the rest of the team and brought some real grit to the side.

Over at Stamford Bridge things had gone from bad to worse. The financial crisis triggered in part by the construction of the East Stand worsened and became very public. Chelsea were in dire financial straits and their form on the pitch was diabolical. Only a month into the season and a few months after the departure of Huddy and myself, Dave Sexton was let go when the team won only two of their opening ten matches. My old friend Ron Suart, a loyal Chelsea servant, was there to steady the ship as caretaker manager, but results didn't improve. When Eddie McCreadie was appointed manager a few matches before the close of the season it was too late. Chelsea finished second from bottom of the division and were relegated for the first time since the days of Ted Drake.

I was surprised at Eddie's appointment – not that he had been offered the job, but that he had taken it. I knew he had taken coaching badges and had considered continuing in football after his playing days were over, but I was unsure whether being the manager of a struggling football club, weighed down with the high expectations of almost everyone and more debt than a Third World country, was the right thing for a man with his complex personality.

Up at Stoke, Alan Hudson proved his influence was not just a flash in the pan as they finished fifth for the second season. Huddy finally broke into the England team, even though Don Revie was manager, and made a memorable debut against West Germany, where we prevailed 1–0. His performance was hailed widely as fantastic, yet Revie only ever played him once again. Like me, he'd been having a few problems with cars and had smashed into a roundabout near his home not once but twice. The newly constructed roundabout is, by all accounts, known locally as the Hudson roundabout to this day.

With Eddie in charge I felt a little more welcome at the Bridge and returned in the early part of the 1975–76 season to stage my testimonial match. The game was a benefit that I was entitled to, having served over ten years with the club, although there were times when I wondered whether it would come off or not. Testimonials are valuable to players as it gives them a lump sum of cash at a time when their careers are often coming to a close and they are looking beyond a life in football. The cheque from the gate receipts of the testimonial has purchased many a pub or other small business for retiring footballers. I was honoured when George Best, now a resident of Chelsea, called and asked if he could play in the game. He was in reality retired by now, although still a young man.

'You will turn up, George?' I had to ask, for George already had a reputation for missing dates for one reason or another. It would have been seen as a con if we had announced that George was playing, the crowds had jammed in to the Bridge, and then he had not shown up. Like one of the Showbiz Eleven charity matches at your local football ground you take the kids to and find the most famous person in the team is a man who wore a Dalek suit in *Dr Who*.

George did turn up and played a blinder alongside Peter Bonetti, Paddy Mulligan, Bert Murray, Peter Houseman, John Hollins, Dave

Me, dive? Frank McClintock, Pat Rice, myself and George Armstrong.
Peter Houseman in the background.

My Jason King phase.

RIGHT: 'This one might not be locked'.
Looking for a way home 1974.

BELOW: Vidal Sassoon cutting my hair.
Why he felt the need to wear football
shorts whilst doing this I cannot
remember.

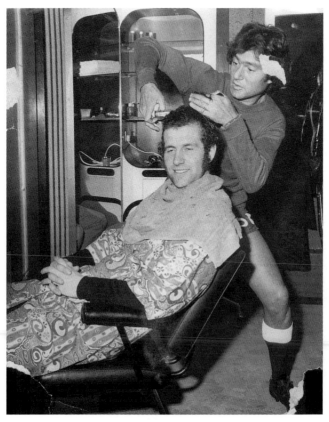

How Dave Sexton could claim I didn't work hard enough in training is beyond me. Steve Kember relaxes alongside.

At Southampton. I am booked for a foul on Phil Holder.
Jim McCalliog and Mick Channon look on.

We won the Cup! Southampton victory run 1976. From L-R: Bobby Stokes, me, Jim McCalliog, Jim Steele, Mick Channon, David Peach, Jim Clooney, Peter Rodrigues and Ian Turner.

My testimonial back at Chelsea. I didn't score as I was too busy counting the crowd. George Best (his only time in a Chelsea shirt), me and Alan Hudson.

With Lynn on our honeymoon.

The family today: Darren, Lynn and me.

Friends Reunited. Alan Hudson is absent as this dinner was to raise money following his horrific car accident. Back Row L-R: David Webb, John Hollins, Ron Stuart, me, Dave Sexton, John Dempsey and Ian Hutchinson (who thought it was fancy dress and came as a waiter). Front Row L-R: Peter Bonetti, Marvin Hinton, Ron Harris, Charlie Cooke and Tommy Baldwin.

Outside the Union Inn, 2002 with my Uncle George
and my co-authors Martin Knight and Martin King.

Webb, George Graham, Jim McCalliog, Keith Weller, Bobby Tambling, Alan Hudson, Chris Garland and Tommy Baldwin. They all generously made the time to form my Peter Osgood's Past Chelsea 11 and we played against the current Chelsea team, which still included Ron Harris, John Dempsey, Charlie Cooke, Hutch and Bill Garner. Young Ray Wilkins captained them. Current Chelsea won a thrilling match 4–3 with Ian Britton, Charlie, Hutch and Bill Garner getting the goals, Bestie himself scoring twice for us and The Sponge grabbing the other. I did not get on the score sheet – I was far too busy doing a head count of the 25,000 crowd in order to roughly calculate the gate receipts. The match has particular significance for Best and Chelsea aficionados because it is the only time that George wore a Chelsea shirt.

The Southampton side was getting better and our form was improving steadily. Lawrie had bought in Mel Blyth from Crystal Palace in defence and, my old mucker from my earliest Chelsea days, Jim McCalliog was now also at the club. Mel used to catch the train to the Dell and while I was banned from driving I boarded the same one. Every day I'd get coffee and toast from the buffet. Every day Mel would eat and drink it and then promptly fall asleep, relying on me to wake him at Southampton. Never once did the tightwad put his hand in his pocket, or even have the courtesy to stay awake and talk to me. He obviously found me very interesting. In the end I got sick of this and one morning left him sleeping on the train. When Lawrie asked me where Mel was I said that he had told me he was taking the day off and continuing the train journey on to Dorset. Lawrie believed me and in a way it was true.

Southampton beat Chelsea 4–1 at the Dell and took a point from them at the Bridge. Eddie asked me around that time whether I would like to come back to Chelsea and we arranged to meet in the Markham Arms, a pub near the ground that had been one of our favourite watering holes. We were just so pleased to be talking, reminiscing and laughing that we didn't get to the nitty-gritty until we were three sheets to the wind. 'Eddie, you just draw up a contract and I'll sign it. I know you'll do your best and see right by me.' And I knew that he would because Eddie is an honest man. Too honest. Although, I was forming a real bond at Southampton the pull of coming home to Chelsea was still strong. It always would be.

My girlfriend Pippa was with me and Eddie that afternoon. Pippa was an air hostess. We met over breakfast in a hotel in Australia – she invited me to a party for cabin crew and it went on from there. A lot of footballers end up marrying trolley dollies and I eventually became one of them. While I was at Southampton we drifted into a relationship which I tried to convince myself was a fling for as long as I could. But when I sorted out a little love nest for our illicit meetings in Lightwater I should have started facing facts. Rose knew something was up but in the beginning she didn't push me about it. Often she viewed me as a big kid, and she still hoped I would grow out of some of my more childish behaviour. Subconsciously, I think, neither of us wanted to broach the subject of my adultery, knowing it might change things forever. In truth neither of us really wanted that. Eventually, though, it came to a head, as these things always do in the end.

Pippa and I were coming back from somewhere or other and heading down the M3 in my beloved 2.5-litre purple Ford Capri, number plate 9 PO, when I came off at the junction for Bagshot and clipped the kerb. The car careered into a field and rolled, not a pleasant experience. We looked at one another and, realising we were still alive, got out of the car. Fortunately there were no other vehicles involved but the car was smashed up, likely to ignite, and I had drunk well over the limit, though I was sobering up fast.

'Act normal,' I commanded. 'Get on the road and walk normally back to the house.' Pippa did this and I leapt a hedge and ran in the opposite direction to The Red Lion, a pub I used a bit. As I poured my first pint down, wondering if the guv'nor was noticing my shaking hand, I could hear the police sirens wailing outside. After three or four more I crept back to the house.

First thing the next morning, assuming the alcohol would be out of my system, I went to Chertsey Police Station and reported the accident. A young copper on the desk seemed pleased to see me. I soon found out why – the incident was all over the papers. 'ENGLAND STAR IN CAR CRASH – MYSTERY BLONDE SEEN RUNNING FROM THE SCENE.' The article did not mention my name, but it did show the number plate of the car, which was a bit of a giveaway. The papers had a lot of fun with that. The young policeman said 'We've been expecting you, Mr Osgood, come this way,' and showed me to an interview room. An older policeman followed and smiled at me.

'Right,' says the young one, 'why did you not report this accident?'

'I thought that was what I was doing now,' I replied. The older policeman caught my eye and without the other one seeing made a zipping motion in front of his mouth. I got the message. 'I have nothing to say until my solicitor arrives.' Which wouldn't be for quite a long time, because I hadn't even contacted him yet. I saw the older policeman in the pub after and it turned out he was a Saints fan. No charges were brought.

Later that morning I took the train down to the Southampton training ground. As I walked into the changing-room Channon's face lit up. 'Who's been a naughty boy then, Ossie?' he says in that rural drawl of his. 'I knews it was you, Ossie, straight away.'

'How's that Mick?'

'Well it says on the radio – England player – off the M3 – and when they were running away the blonde was 30 yards in front of the footballer.'

The dressing-room erupted.

But it wasn't at all funny when I had to come clean with Rose. She read the papers. It was the hardest thing I have ever done, before or since. My boys were eight and ten and I felt like shit tearing the family apart. This truly was the hangover after the party. The price of gallivanting and leading the high life. Amid tears all round I walked out of the family home and moved in with my pal Dave near the Dell, commuting between there and Lightwater. The sheer misery of it all weighed down on me. I could not concentrate, my game was bad, my training was half-hearted and I was drinking more than usual to block it all out. I didn't want to be away from Rose and the kids but Pippa was like a drug that I couldn't give up. Like the proverbial ostrich, I buried my head in the sand and hoped things would work themselves through.

Lawrie McMenemy was so concerned that he summoned me to his house to sort things out. When I arrived Rose was sitting in the room, red-eyed and forlorn, with Lawrie's wife Anne. What had I done to this poor woman? The young innocent girl who thought that by marrying a local bricklayer (who happened to be good at football) she'd lead a life much the same as her mum and dad before her? We aired our feelings and emotions ran high. Lawrie had hoped that getting us together, with him and his wife acting as referees and counsellors, would help resolve the situation. But I left Chandler's Ford even more confused and upset than when I arrived. My head was like a pressure cooker. I even harboured silly thoughts about getting a transfer to some club on the other side of the world and escaping from all of it. After months of toing and froing between my friend's house, Pippa's place and the family home, I finally moved in with Pippa. But I have to say that the only time I felt my head was clear and I was relatively relaxed was when Pippa was away flying and I could get in the car and go and see Rose and the kids.

I hate decisions, much preferring other people to make them for me – at least then I can blame them when things go wrong – but there was no one to blame other than myself for the situation I found myself in. From playing for England only months before, I was now playing in the wilderness of the Second Division and the club I loved, Chelsea, was falling apart at the seams. My marriage was in shreds and Rose was blameless in all of it. I had rarely been at home for years, did exactly what suited me, and when I wanted, and left her to raise the kids with hardly any emotional support. I knew what I was doing was wrong but, at times, it was like watching someone else's life unfurl in front of me.

The talks with Eddie never progressed mainly, I guess, because he couldn't persuade the board to make an offer for me. Indeed, money was so tight at the club that Eddie and some players had taken a pay cut. But also the Saints were going great guns in the FA Cup and my mind was firmly fixed on seeing the run out. Before I knew it we were in the semi-finals and playing Crystal Palace at Stamford Bridge of all places. Palace were now in the Third Division, but you would never have known it. Malcolm Allison was in charge and he made more waves than all of the First Division managers put together. He created an excitement at the club you could almost touch. Talented players like Alan Whittle, Peter Taylor and Don Rogers thrilled the crowd and blended well with some upcoming home-grown talent. That day Malcolm fixed his enduring image in the public consciousness by walking onto the pitch with his fur coat, fedora hat and a cigar so big it would make Monica Lewinsky wince. He invited me to move to Selhurst Park, and with my old friend Ray Bloye backing the club he had the funds to buy me, but having just started to adjust and accept Second Division football the thought of running out in the Third filled me with dread. We beat Palace 2–0, and then it sank in – I was going back to Wembley for an FA Cup final. It had the potential to be a fairy-tale match, for we were one of the few Second Division clubs to make the FA Cup final in modern times and we were pitched against a now rejuvenated, young Manchester United side. Manager? Tommy Docherty.

The synergy in football always amazes and excites me. If I were a gambling man (and fortunately that is one of the few vices open to young footballers that I did not succumb to) I would look for the synergy bet. For example, what odds would you have got on Alan Hudson to score the first goal when he returned to the Bridge that first time with Stoke? Or for Denis Law to score the goal for Manchester City that relegated his old club Manchester United? Or for Terry Venables' Spurs to defeat his old boss Tommy Docherty's Chelsea in the 1967 Cup final? There's a synergy story in every big match and if you stuck to betting on those, I'm sure you'd win more than you'd lose. That's what makes football such a wonderful game – the potential for the meek to overcome the mighty, the possibility of righting wrong and exacting a bit of revenge, and the opportunity for loved players or managers to turn it on, on the big stage one last time and maybe nick an honour when everyone thought all was lost.

The week after the Palace game, we played up at Grimsby in a pedestrian Second Division league game. However, a couple of thousand Southampton fans were going to be making the trip to salute the team for making it through to the final. On the Friday night Channon invited us all to his hotel room.

'This is the best time of my life and I thinks we should be celebrating,' he reasoned. He wasn't really a drinker but he was determined to mark the occasion. I'm not proud of it, but we staggered out of Mick's room at five in the morning. Legless. All of us. There's always a grass in the camp and someone told Lawrie. Understandably he was furious. As we sat in the dressing-room, some of us openly nursing our sore heads, he dressed us down something rotten.

'You lads should be ashamed of yourselves. There are 2,000 fans out there who have travelled all the way from home to see you boys. You know why? Because they are so fucking proud of you. And how do you repay them? You all go drinking all night and leave yourselves unfit to play. Shame on you!'

We did feel bad, but physically we could not raise ourselves to play in the first half. There were probably more back and sideways passes in that 45 minutes than in that entire season. We were dead lucky to traipse in for half-time at 0–0. Lawrie was waiting for us. His temper had not improved.

'I can't even look at you. I'm not even sure I want to be your manager.' He shook his head and sat down. We'd never seen him this upset.

'Don't worry Gaffer, we won't let you down,' piped up Channon. He was always the optimist. Scans the papers every day to see if they've found Glenn Miller.

'You've already let me down,' Lawrie sighed.

In the second half Mick Channon went out and duly scored four goals. His hangover must have lifted. Bobby Stokes got the other in a 5–0 drubbing. Back in the dressing-room Lawrie couldn't conceal a grin.

'You lucky, lucky bastards.'

'Gaffer, I'm telling you,' Channon chirps, 'if the lager hadn't run out at 5 o' clock we'd have won 9–0, no sweat.'

The week before the final Lawrie booked us all in to The Selsdon Park Hotel, a tranquil venue nestled in the Surrey countryside. His strategy was low-key, all about relaxing us and banishing any thoughts that we were no-hoper Second Division underdogs. We knew we had a good chance anyway. We were playing well together and worked hard as a team. United were a young side with many new players and the pressure would be on them to snuff us out, but as everyone knows, over 90 minutes anything can happen.

We trained very lightly during the week and played some golf. On the Thursday night Lawrie said that those of us who wanted to go out on the town were welcome to. I remember Jim McCalliog and Jim Steele took up the offer, but unusually for me, I decided to decline. The match was becoming more and more important to me as each day rolled by. I was determined that my career at Southampton was not going to become a mere footnote in football history. 'Osgood did actually play at Wembley one last time . . . but he was ineffective in the massive defeat against a dynamic Manchester United . . .' No thanks.

Walking out at Wembley is the most incredible feeling. I find it hard to put it into words. In the dressing-room you cannot hear the crowd at all, and as you walk down the tunnel it is not until you are practically passing out that you glimpse the crowd and start to hear the din. Then as you emerge into the sunlight your senses are literally assaulted by the deafening roar around the stadium and the mass of colour. The atmosphere is truly electric. Not manufactured like the palaver that accompanies baseball matches in America, for example, but pure raw excitement. Anticipation and a general goodwill pulses around the stadium. The sense of history and occasion embraces you. For 90 minutes at least (and longer if you win) the world is a lovely place and you are the very centre of it. I have never taken drugs in my life, but if users get just 10 per cent of the rush that I got from playing in an FA Cup final at Wembley then I can sort of understand what keeps them going back.

Playing for United that day was Alex Stepney (who had had a short spell at Chelsea in the 1960s) in goal, Gordon Hill (who for a time was described as the wonder boy of English football) and Martin Buchan, their Scottish captain. I once heard Buchan talking on TV. He was asked how many caps he won. 'Half as many as I should have,' he replied. Obviously Martin Buchan's greatest fan was Martin Buchan. It wasn't a brilliant match from the neutral's point of view, but it was heavenly for us because thanks to a super goal from little Bobby Stokes in the 82nd minute we won the game 1–0. United's protests that the goal was offside were to no avail. Lawrie had been as good as his word. Within a couple of years, he had assured me at our first meeting, Southampton would be challenging for major honours. We were, and winning them too. Granted, the drop into the Second Division was not in the plan, but as we did the lap of honour at five o' clock that scorching hot day in May 1976 no one doubted Lawrie McMenemy any more. I was only sorry that my mum and dad were not at the stadium to see it and savour the moment, but Dad's health had been failing for some time and the trip would have been too much for the old man. I knew all the family would be crowded around the television set watching at home. As we came down the famous Wembley steps after collecting our medals and the cup, Bobby Stokes passed me the trophy and I could see the BBC TV camera fixed firmly on me. I got up close and mouthed slowly, so there could be no mistake, 'Dad, this is for you.'

In 1973 when I joined the Saints as manager, I knew I had to rebuild the team by blending youth with experience. I'd always admired the skills of Peter Osgood and when I heard he was having a problem with Chelsea I made a bid and bought him. It was seen as a gamble at the time but he proved to be a joy to work with and I never had any off-field problems with him. In fact all the young players at the club like the Wallace brothers, Steve Williams and Steve Moran, looked up to him. He played an integral part in our FA Cup win over Southampton.

In a game against Portsmouth our centre-half came off injured and Ossie indicated to me that he would switch roles and play at the back. This he did with great effect, laying out their big bruiser of a centre-forward within minutes. The crowd howled at him but Ossie just waved and smiled. The most graceful thing I ever saw him do was trap a ball with his shoulder blades, let it drop to his feet and then hit an inch perfect 40-yard pass to one of our forwards. Pure magic.

L. McMenemy, Football Manager

12

Osgood was Good

I SAW TOMMY IMMEDIATELY AFTER THE GAME, AND HE WAS CRUSHED. 'DON'T worry, Boss,' I said, 'you'll be back next year.' He was, beating Liverpool and now, nearly 40 years after he first became my manager, I still call him Boss.

Our celebrations, like our build-up, were fairly low key. We went to a cabaret in London and then on to the Talk of the Town. I was disappointed, to be honest. We were in London and all those wonderful fans who had travelled to Wembley were naturally back in Southampton. At a historical time like this team and fans should be together. I spent the night with Rose and the boys in Windsor and then on Sunday, after having a drink with all the family, drove down to Southampton where the celebrations were in full flow. I had to run through the gathered crowds to hop onto the victory bus as it dawdled through the city to the Guildhall, soaking up the adoration. I plonked down, out of breath, next to Lawrie who had a bottle of champagne between his legs on the floor and another in his hand. Not bad for a man who was the advertising face of alcohol-free Kaliber lager at the time. As we toasted the crowds from the balcony of the Guildhall I marvelled at how things had turned out. If nothing else, football, like life, keeps surprising you.

A couple of months later the team were guests of honour at the Tiberius gambling club in Southampton. The FA Cup was on display. As the drink flowed a prank developed in my mind and I bet a couple of the lads I could steal the cup and get it out the building. It was easy to do. After the dinner had finished I simply went back into the club and sought out the security man. I gave him a story about having to have some impromptu photos done with the cup and said I would bring it back as soon as I was finished. The guard was only too pleased to release it. Once I got out into the car park and showed it to Jim Steele and David Peach I wasn't sure what to do with it, so I bundled it unceremoniously into the boot of the car. We drove into the city centre and stopped by a mobile burger van for a coffee and a hot dog. By now the pubs were chucking out and a fair-sized, boisterous crowd had gathered around us. 'Hang on a minute lads, I've got something for you,' said Jim. He went to the boot and to their shock, but great amusement, pulled out the instantly recognisable FA Cup. Everyone started to chuck their coffees and teas into it, and we passed the cup around and everyone drank from it. Even the girls. Eventually I drove home and took the cup inside with me, leaving it on the sideboard whilst I crawled into bed.

In the morning I awoke with a hangover. Then fear in the pit of my stomach when I remembered that the FA Cup was downstairs next to my car keys, loose change and screwed-up fivers on the sideboard. For all I knew, Pickles the dog was out looking for it at that very moment. I grabbed it, ran to the car and sped off to the Dell. I nipped in the door, rushed up to Lawrie's office, placed the cup quietly by his door and then ran back downstairs and got changed for training. Three minutes later I was summoned to the office. Lawrie was at his desk looking at me very sternly, with Ted Bates, Mr Southampton, standing behind him, arms folded, looking down at the floor. The cup was on the desk. They couldn't keep up the pretence for more than a few seconds. Both men broke into broad smiles. 'You've pulled some strokes in your time, bonny lad, but this takes the biscuit. The secretary has practically had a heart attack. But I told him you'd have it and it would be safe. Go on, be off with you.' Back in the changing-room the lads were all grinning from ear to ear, and they gave me a round of applause.

Even though we won the Cup, possibly *because* we won the Cup, we failed to secure promotion to the First Division, finishing sixth. I had scored a respectable 21 goals, had played well in the final and was pleased when the critics praised my contribution to the Southampton story, saying that Lawrie's decision to sign me was inspired and that I was displaying a new, more mature side to my game. Meanwhile Chelsea finished mid-table in the Second Division but sensibly did not sack Eddie for failing to take them straight back into the top flight, instead allowing him time to rebuild the side around the youth in the club. They had little choice, as there was no money to buy players. The team that ended the season included only Ron Harris and Bill Garner from my era, and Bill was a late joiner. Ray Wilkins was rapidly developing into a world-class player and if they could hold onto him and bring on the likes of Gary Stanley, Kenny Swain, Ray Lewington and Stevie Finniston I thought Eddie had a good chance of bringing the glory days back to Stamford Bridge.

The following season, 1976–77, was an anti-climax for Southampton fans and players because we failed to be promoted again; in fact we only finished mid-table. Time was definitely running out for me, as I had now hit 30 years of age – a big psychological turning point for strikers in the highest levels of the game. While goalkeepers can keep going until their late 30s and defenders and some midfielders to their mid-30s, it is rare for forwards to survive much after their early 30s. I was now beginning to accept that I might not play in the First Division again, let alone win further honours.

This season really just marked time for Southampton, but back at the Bridge, Eddie had triumphantly taken Chelsea back into the First Division much to the delight of the fans, now proudly calling themselves 'Eddie McCreadie's Blue and White Army'. My two teams met in the FA Cup third round that season. Channon scored a goal for Southampton at The Dell that forced a replay, I remember him celebrating in his inimitable style, doing the Pete Townshend windmill movement with his arm. At the Bridge we won 3–0, but we were not to go much further in the competition.

Channon was not as generous with his passes as the people I was used to playing off, like Hutch and Tommy. Quite early in my time with Southampton I decided to tackle him on the subject. 'Mick, how come you hardly ever pass to me?'

He looked at me and grinned. 'Ossie,' he said, 'when I sees the whites of them posts, nothing else matters. I just have to go for it.' Sometimes I'd look at Mick and watch him laughing to himself and muttering. I'm sure he was slightly mad.

The boys off the field were proving harder to break-up than the old Chelsea team on the field. Even though some of us had moved on and were residing at different ends of the country we reconvened as often as we could. Inevitably it would be at Alexandres the restaurant run by Camillo and Manuel. Huddy would come down from Stoke, me up from Southampton, Webby over from QPR and those who were still at the club, like Hutch and Eddie, from across the road. One time Huddy had bought down a couple of the Stoke players. They were out and out northerners and were not happy about us being comfortable with Camillo and Manuel, who were outrageously camp. One insisted that there were no homosexuals in northern England and, honest to God, sat with his back to the wall. That was until he had had a bottle of wine or three. Earlier in the afternoon he had asked me to accompany him to the toilet for safety, a few hours later he was walking around waving his manhood about. 'Come on then Camillo,' he taunted, 'get some of this.' When Camillo dived under the table to get some of that his eyes crossed and he yelped as we heard Camillo's jaw lock.

We all reunited again in March of 1977 for the most tragic of reasons. It's funny how one telephone call can change your life. Actually, there's nothing funny about it. I got a call one Sunday afternoon, and for the life of me I cannot recall from whom, such was the shock. Peter Houseman is dead, I was told. Peter had left Chelsea too by then and was playing in the Third Division for Oxford United. He, his wife Sally and another couple were coming home from a function when their car collided with another. All four adults were killed, leaving six orphans between them. He had played against Crystal Palace that very day and typically in the evening had attended a fund-raising event. Peter was not driving. I'm not sure he could drive even then. I know he used to turn up to training and matches having travelled on the tube. I racked my brain to recall when I had last seen him, what our last words had been, chastised myself for not picking up the phone and calling him more often. Peter was the quiet one, he never got the hump, and you didn't have to worry about him because he was so steady. We called him Nobby; some of the fans called him Mary, an unfair reference, I think, to his style of playing. He was never a great imbiber but never judged us for our lifestyle and youthful indiscretions. He smiled and laughed a lot and sometimes shook his head. He had a sense of humour all right, but he also had his life to lead. He was like the kid at school that wanted to have the crack but had his A levels to be getting on with. He knew we loved him though, I'm sure, and I know he loved us. I rang a few people, some had heard, a couple hadn't. The sharing of the news delays dealing with it initially at a time like that. There was no one in his family to call to offer condolences. I couldn't contact the devastated young children. It really was awful. I thought back to that day, a lifetime ago, when we were barely shaving, and I was making my first debut for the youth side. The lads took the piss out of me over my scruffy dress and he smiled and reassured me. No one else knew he had done it. That was Nobby. It's true – the good really do die young.

The lads all turned up for the funeral. It was a sombre affair. For some reason we avoided each other's eyes. This wasn't in the plan. If one of us was going to go first it was never going to be Nobby. We assembled in a pub near the church and exchanged some small talk. Our handshakes that day were heartfelt but none of us knew what to say. Eventually I lifted my glass and said quietly, 'To Peter.'

'To Peter,' they chorused.

I don't know if the others felt it but it was then I realised that we were an entity beyond a football team. That we were destined to be part of each other's lives, to varying degrees, for the rest of them. Even then we were having our bust-ups, rows and huffs. We still do. But the bond between us is stronger than any of these diversions, and at the end of the day we all look out for each other. Talking to other ex-players, there seems to be no other team that are still in so much contact, 30 or so years after its break-up.

We played a testimonial to raise money for Peter's and his friends' orphaned children and nearly 17,000 turned up to see a 1970 XI play the current Chelsea team. Everyone wanted to take part. The Cat was in goal, Ron and Eddie were the full-backs, Johnny Boyle, Johnny Hollins, Webby, Marvin Hinton and Huddy in the middle of the park and me, Tommy, Alan Birchenall and Hutch up front. Even good old Alan Ball put in a guest appearance. Nobby would have been pleased. God rest him.

Before the 1977–78 season started it went boss-eyed for Chelsea. Eddie Mac justifiably felt that his achievement entitled him to negotiate a new contract with the club, and he particularly wanted a company car. I'm sure no other First Division manager had to suffer the indignity of not having one at the time, financial difficulties or no financial difficulties. The bloke who came to sell them toilet paper had a company car, for God's sake. Chelsea wouldn't or couldn't play ball, having just negotiated breathing space with Chelsea's creditors. However, if he had really wanted to, I believe he could have swung it. The only chance the creditors of the club had of getting their money back would be for the club to achieve success again, and Eddie had just proved he was capable of delivering that. To lay out another

£6,000 for a car was a small price to pay to keep the momentum going but the club saw it differently. Eddie McCreadie was not a greedy man, but he was no mug either. He resigned and wandered off into the football wilderness, never to be seen again. A great shame.

By the start of the 1977–78 season Lawrie was breaking up the Cup-winning side and had already brought in Alan Ball, Ted McDougall and Phil Boyer, I sensed my days at the Dell were numbered. I was 31 and understandably I probably did not figure in the manager's long-term plans. This was underlined when he sent me up to Norwich City on a month's loan. I was pleasantly surprised to find that it was a smashing set-up and enjoyed myself immensely. At least, against the run of play, I was playing back in the First Division. John Bond was the manager and he really was a good coach, reminded me a lot of Dave Sexton. He had Graham Paddon, a real Norwich favourite, and Martin Peters, ex-West Ham, Tottenham and England, enjoying an Indian summer in the side. At the end of my loan period John Bond asked Lawrie if he could extend the loan but Lawrie replied, 'Buy him or he's coming back down here.'

'Tell Lawrie you want to extend the loan,' John asked me after we had just finished playing at Everton.

'No, I best go back to Southampton,' I said.

'In that case you can make your own way home.' John got on the team coach, signalling for the driver to close the doors behind him. It was for real. I couldn't believe it.

Back at the Dell things had picked up considerably; we were top of the Second Division after 16 games and promotion this time around looked pretty assured. I slipped back into the first team and was feeling pretty pleased with myself after scoring in a match against Leyton Orient and their underrated goalkeeper John Jackson. He had almost single-handedly kept Crystal Palace in the First Division for a few seasons. I was really happy, especially now Bally had arrived. Like me he was by now an old hand in the football game and the two of us let any pressure wash over us and just got on with enjoying ourselves.

One afternoon after training Bally, myself and a couple of other lads took a bottle of champagne into the sauna and settled back for a relaxing drink and chat. One of the younger players opened the door and said, 'Lawrie wants to see you, Alan, in the office.'

'Tell him I'm busy, tell him to come down here.' Bally wasn't being bolshy, he enjoyed a good relationship with the manager; he was simply winding him up. After a while the door swung open and in walked Lawrie in his customary suit, collar and tie. In his hand was a new bottle of champagne. 'If you can't beat 'em, join 'em,' he grunted and proceeded to share the bottle with us without even loosening his tie. As he discussed his business with Alan the perspiration formed in a puddle around him.

Thinking about Alan Ball reminds me of a curious incident with Brian Clough. Southampton had played up at Nottingham Forest and when the game ended I really fancied a drink so I cantered off the pitch, straight into the shower and was dressed before the other lads had even got their boots off. I headed upstairs to the players' bar and ordered myself a lager. There was no one in there I knew until Mr Clough himself came marching in. Marching is the right word. When he entered, conversations tailed off and people stood aside, so his path to the bar was unencumbered. When he saw me he looked me up and down. 'Young man, what do you think you are doing here?'

'Having a drink, Mr Clough.'

'Oh no you're not, Osgood. Your sort are not welcome here.' He pushed my glass away from me on the bar and motioned for the barman to pick it up.

'Are you serious?' I was amazed, but I knew he was and that if I argued there would be a terrible scene. I could imagine him grabbing me by the scruff of the neck and throwing me out. If I had retaliated and the press had got hold of it, who would have been the troublemaker? Peter Osgood or Brian Clough OBE? So, angry and thoroughly embarrassed, I left the bar. I don't know what his problem was. I have no recall of ever exchanging a cross word with him and have only ever expressed admiration for his management record. I put it down to him being pissed. With the benefit of hindsight and now knowing about self-confessed problems with drink, I wonder if he was under the influence that day.

Later, Southampton were in Torremelinos and they ran into the Forest team, who were out there for the same reason – a pre-season tour of Mediterranean drinking establishments. Alan Ball and Ted McDougall were sitting around the pool of the hotel downing a few cold lagers when Clough himself came down and sat on a table close to them. Bally was reminded of the incident with me. He called across to him, 'Oy Clough, anyone ever told you what a wanker you are?'

'I beg your pardon?' Even Cloughie was momentarily tongue-tied.

'I would never have played for you in a million years,' continued Bally.

'And I, my son, would never have had you in one of my teams.'

Before the argument could develop further Lawrie McMenemy arrived in the bar area.

'I have just been insulted by one of your senior players,' Clough complained.

'In what way?'

'Ball over there called me a wanker.'

Lawrie shrugged his shoulders and kept walking, making Brian Clough look about a foot tall.

Even though I was enjoying myself and Southampton's prospects were looking up, when my occasional agent Ken Adams approached me and told me that America beckoned I could not help feeling excited. It is easy to forget just how big the American game was going to be. Once the Yanks decided they were going to introduce football (or soccer as they preferred to call it to avoid confusion with American football) it was like a gold rush. We moan nowadays about mercenary foreign footballers coming to our shores, but once the Americans declared that soccer was going to become their new national game, you couldn't move in Heathrow Terminal Four for twilight English footballers eager to grab a slice of the cake. I was at the front of the queue. The newly formed Philadelphia Furies had said they were interested in me, or who knows, more likely Ken Adams had said I was interested in them. All they wanted were big names to kick-start the soccer industry and maybe start to blood their young generation in this entirely new sport. Rodney Marsh, for one, was so confident that this was the future of international football. He was very dismissive about the prospects of the English game before he flew off to join Tampa Bay Rowdies. Rodney and I didn't see eye to eye. Once I was having what I thought was a constructive debate with him over footballing tactics. 'You don't know what you're talking about Ossie,' he snorted dismissively.

'Everyone's entitled to an opinion, Rodney.'

'Put your caps and medals on the table,' he challenged. If he was a Mars Bar Rodney Marsh would eat himself.

I spoke to Lawrie; he was absolutely confident of promotion to the First Division (and he was to be proved correct) and offered me a two-year contract. But I was excited by the prospect of being a pioneer in the States, tempted by the lifestyle on offer and convinced by the money on the table, so we parted on the best of terms. I signed for the Philadelphia Furies and Pippa and I packed our bags as quickly as that for a new life Stateside. Before long, half the big names of the 1960s and early '70s were following suit. George Best, Franz Beckenbauer, Johann Cruyff and Pele had all signed for the New York Cosmos, Rodney was down in Florida with Tampa Bay, Alan Hudson eventually found his way to Seattle Sounders and hosts of other familiar names were dotted around the United States. For a short while many English Second and Third Division players upped sticks and found themselves much bigger fish in a much smaller pond.

I made a promotional video for the Furies. It had all the production values of a Hollywood movie. It would, wouldn't it? They had me running up the steps of a prestigious building mimicking a scene from one of the *Rocky* films, crossing the Benjamin Franklin Bridge, leaping fences and flying through the air. It was a stylish piece of work and to my regret I no longer have a copy of it. It was adopted as the promotional film for this new American industry and was even shown on the *News at Ten* back at home.

The whole US soccer experience was great, but after a while you had to adjust to the fact that you had signed up to the entertainment industry, or you got out. My club was financially backed by Paul Simon and members of the Yes rock group among others. Although the American people embraced the concept with enthusiasm, like many of the ageing stars out there it had no legs. Once you'd been to see this George Best or Pele everyone talks about – well, that was it. There was no history or passion to sustain it. Only the biggest of clashes drew in substantial crowds and although we were stars in our home countries we were pretty insignificant out there. No one really cared who won or lost and because of the vast geographical spread there was no such thing as a travelling fan base – matches had to be played as part of tours. Therefore the atmosphere at games was pure theatre. Someone famously said it was a circus and it was. When the crowd cheered when a goal was scored I couldn't help thinking of canned laughter.

The final straw for me was when we were playing a match against Fort Lauderdale. Alan Ball was guesting in the team and as we stood out on the pitch kicking the ball aimlessly to each other before the game we wondered where our opponents were. We soon found out. Suddenly we heard all this whooping and hollering and a wagon train pulled by horses emerged from a gate onto the pitch. The Fort Lauderdale players jumped off their carriages in their football kit, wearing large cowboy hats and dancing around like madmen, shooting blanks into the air. I looked at Bally and shook my head. 'That's my fucking lot. I'm going home.'

It wasn't that I was particularly unhappy; I had been under no illusions about what to expect. I could see that it would be a long haul and I could also see that pure economics meant that sooner or later most of us would be homeward bound. An injury picked up on astro-turf didn't help, but I was really missing Rose and the kids too and after nine months of American sunshine, Pippa and I packed our bags again and returned to England. The American dream had not quite turned into a nightmare, but I had woken up.

Autumn 1978. For the first time in my life I was unemployed and not playing football. I was coming up to 32 years of age and the reality of my situation hit me like a fist in the face. I had made no preparations for my post-playing career whatsoever. I had no prospects or serious inclination to go into coaching or management, and no business interests outside the game. Rose and the boys quite rightly had the family home. Pippa and I had the small place in Lightwater, but that was as far as my assets went. I had some money in the bank but before long I was to find out painfully how quickly your bank balance reduces once the monthly pay cheque ceases. Welcome back to the real world, Ossie.

Chelsea had replaced Eddie McCreadie with another ex-defender, Ken Shellito, as manager but their first season back in the First Division had been disappointing, with them finishing 16th. Brian Clough's Nottingham Forest were riding high as League Champions, the second time now that he had taken a lowly Second Division side to these heights. By November of the 1978–79 season Chelsea had won only twice in the League, and they already looked doomed to drop back into the Second Division. I received a call from Ken asking me if I wanted to come back to the Bridge. I didn't think long and hard about it, but perhaps I should have. 'You'll have to talk to Philadelphia,' I told him, as they still held my contract. Ken swiftly agreed a £25,000 fee with them and before I knew it, I was back in employment, back in the game and back at Chelsea. When I had started at Chelsea I was cleaning Ken Shellito's boots – now I would be licking them.

I hadn't been gone five years yet, but it seemed an age. I had won an FA Cup, played in the Second Division and pioneered the game in America in the meantime. The team I had left was basically still the one that had won the FA Cup in 1970 and the European Cup-Winners' Cup in 1971. Now only Ron Harris and Peter Bonetti survived. My last league game for the Blues had been against Liverpool in December of 1973 and 33,000 had watched us at Stamford Bridge. My second debut was away to Middlesbrough at the old Ayresome Park ground and only 15,000 were in attendance. The good news was that I got on the score sheet, the bad news was that we were hammered 7–2. Chelsea fans were up there in good numbers, which was nice to see, and they gave me a fantastic welcome. I did feel I'd come home at last. I made up my mind that day that whatever happened I wanted to finish my career with Chelsea, the club I started with.

The wonderful thing about Chelsea fans was their loyal support, and especially their away following. People rave about the Manchester United and Liverpool fans, but these two clubs won trophies regularly. Chelsea fans really had little reward for their loyalty other than the 1955 League Championship, now a fading memory, and the burst of glory at the turn of the decade. It sometimes seemed that the harder the going got the more the Chelsea crowd dug their heels in. Support-wise we have been one of the top five clubs ever since I can remember, yet our trophy-winning record nowhere near reflects that. I cannot overstress the wonder we all felt when we'd turn up at Sheffield for an evening game on a cold winter's night, for example, and the ground was packed three out of four sides with Chelsea. It was remarkable. There was a great sense of sharing the battle together. The boys became a bit boisterous, especially after Chelsea fell into the Second Division in the 1970s for the first time, but we tended to turn a blind eye to what might or might not be going down on the terraces. Although when we were getting stick on the pitch and the local crowd were spitting on our backs as we took the throw-ins, we couldn't help smiling inwardly, picturing their faces when they left at the end of the match and found the Shed Boys waiting outside for them. That day at Middlesbrough springs to mind. One minute we were facing hostility from the home end and the next the whole terrace seemed to be cheering us on. Something funny was going on.

Now there was a nastier edge in football generally creeping in. It hit me at Chelsea when I came back. Not so much the undercurrent of crowd violence, but more that the fun seemed to have taken a back seat. A great deal was at stake, the press had become merciless and the average tenure of a manager was becoming shorter and shorter. To become England manager you had to have a skin thicker than a docker's sandwich. Players seemed to be taking themselves more seriously and the gulf between them and the paying fans was widening by the day. The abuse from the crowd had lost the humour it once had and was often positively scary. Chopper, as usual, managed to move with the times. In one game a chap by the corner flag screamed at him 'You're a c**t, Harris!'

Ron turned round and grinned at him. 'You're a bigger one, 'cos you're paying my wages, my son.'

Although Ken Shellito had signed me, he had barely welcomed me back through the door before he was carrying his bin liner stuffed with his belongings out of it. He hadn't been sacked but had resigned. The results were still abominable and the fact that the chairman was openly courting Miljan Miljanic, the Yugoslav coach, undermined him. I don't know if Frank Upton had been officially appointed as his replacement, but no sooner had Ken walked out the door than it was announced that he was in charge. Frank had played for Chelsea under the Doc and was part of the early '60s promotion side. Recently he had returned as a member of the backroom staff. He gathered us all together and made a little speech.

'I'm in charge now. So no more Frank, from now on you call me Boss.'

Here we go, I thought. Lunatics, asylums and takeovers entered my head.

Literally a day later we all heard that Danny Blanchflower had been offered the job and had accepted. When we walked out on the training ground I made a point of shouting, 'All right Frank?'

By the time of my second debut for Chelsea Danny Blanchflower was in situ. It was a curious appointment. Danny had captained the legendary Tottenham Double-winning side of the early 1960s and had been a bedrock of the Northern Ireland international team for many years. He remained one the most respected and well-liked men in the game, but had been more or less out of it for many years, making his living from journalism, and semi-retired. His appointment was akin to Neil Kinnock being reinstated as leader of the Labour Party now, with all the water that has gone under that particular bridge. He was a lovely man with his quiet lilting Irish accent, but he wanted to play the push-and-run football epitomised by that Tottenham side he had captained nearly 20 years before. It was inappropriate.

Results didn't improve. We lost 3–0 to Manchester United (now managed by Dave Sexton) at Old Trafford in the FA Cup third round.

Dave was on the up again and his reputation in the game just kept improving as time went by. There was a flicker of hope when we beat their neighbours, Manchester City, a few days later 3–2 in an entertaining and exciting match at Maine Road. Channon was now in their side, as was Brian Kidd, the ex-United man, whom I had played with in the England Under-23s over a decade before. We didn't look bad that day. I scored, along with Clive Walker and Duncan McKenzie. That was to be my last goal for Chelsea.

Clive became a firm favourite at Chelsea and was remarkably still playing senior football up until very recently. Duncan McKenzie could be brilliant on his day, but like his employers at that particular time had trouble in sustaining it. The next week we beat Birmingham, with Ray Wilkins scoring both goals, but there the revival ended. I was dropped and the team limped home bottom of the First Division. The two things were not connected. I knew in my heart now that my legs had gone and therefore my pace.

My penultimate game for Chelsea was a 1–1 draw at Stamford Bridge with Arsenal. We knew we were down and I tried to savour the occasion, for I was reasonably sure that this would be my final game before a big crowd in a London derby. I would never dismiss the capability of the game to throw up the most unlikely opportunities, but I had probably had my share of them by then. It was a sunny day and that Arsenal side boasted Pat Jennings, another survivor from the 1960s, the magical Liam Brady, hot-shot Malcolm Macdonald and David O'Leary. The Shed were in full song, rallying around the team even though we'd been relegated. They sang 'Born is the King of Stamford Bridge', and I stood for a minute with my hands on my hips, just looking at them and smiling. I wanted to climb in there and hug each and every one of them. Say thank you for making my life special.

In the close season we played an exhibition match abroad and coincidentally Southampton were out there at the same time. We all palled up and had one good evening where everyone got nicely drunk. The pleasant vibes soon dissipated when I saw Brian O' Neil standing on tiptoe, whispering into Mickey Droy's ear. Mickey kept looking over at me. Now, Mickey was a lump and a half. He lumbered over to me and said, 'Brian says you said I look like Frankenstein's monster.' Very playground, I know, but these things do seem important to you I suppose when you've had 16 pina coladas.

'Don't be silly Mickey, why would I say that?'

Brian O'Neil probably thought this was a good practical joke, but

Mickey was not seeing the funny side and when I realised that, neither was I. I was a big lad but Mickey seemed to tower over me. His fists were like hams and he had a jaw that looked like it had been hewn from granite. Ignoring my protestations he insisted we go outside into the evening sun. More out of panic than anything else, I hit him with everything I had before he could do the same to me. It was a good shot. To my surprise and slight horror he toppled over. I then fell on him, hoping I could stop him getting up. Fortunately before he could all the lads ran out, broke up the fight and kept us apart. When we sobered up we couldn't believe that we had both been so stupid.

I made it through to the next season, 1979–80. Geoff Hurst had joined as coach but Danny Blanchflower was still in charge. Just. The start of the new season didn't look too bad, even though Ray Wilkins, the jewel in our battered crown, had finally put himself in front of his ailing club and moved to Manchester United. We won two and drew one in the first three games and I could see that Danny and Geoff could work together. Their strengths and weaknesses complemented one another. Geoff was more in touch with the modern game tactically. Danny was better at handling the players, especially the older ones.

My very last real game in a Chelsea shirt was on 8 September 1979. We lost 2–1 at home to Birmingham. Mickey Droy had assumed the captaincy and I was substituted for Gary Chivers. The Birmingham match had followed defeats to Newcastle in the league and Plymouth in the League Cup. After that game Danny Blanchflower resigned and Geoff jumped into his very warm seat. I knew Geoff well, had roomed with him in Mexico and liked him, but Danny was not treated well and I believe Geoff contributed to that situation by sitting back and not helping Danny when he knew he was struggling. I saw Danny as he was leaving and the sadness in his eyes upset me. 'I'm sorry Peter,' he said as he shook my hand. 'I just wasn't up to the job.'

'Don't be silly, Gaffer, You didn't have the raw material to work with.' And there was a bit of truth in both statements.

With Danny gone there was little point in trying to build a manager/player relationship with Geoff Hurst. We were nearly the same age. Geoff didn't approve of my lifestyle, imagined or real. When he was getting pictured in the local paper opening fêtes, Charlie, the boys and me would be in the beer tent chucking lager down our necks. He knew I spoke my mind and probably believed that I would be a threat to his authority. In his autobiography he says he had to fine me for being late for training and was faced with the task of easing me out of the club. I don't remember it that way. He named his first team squad and I was number 16. I wasn't sure whether to read too much into that or not, but I went to see him about it. Fittingly, a song called 'We Don't Talk Any More' by Cliff Richard was at the top of the charts. Mrs Thatcher had been in office for only a few months and Trevor Francis had just become the first £1m footballer.

'You stabbed a great man in the back,' was my rather direct opening, referring to Danny Blanchflower.

Geoff shuffled awkwardly in his seat across the desk from me. I couldn't help thinking that he didn't look right in a suit sitting behind a big desk.

'If you don't like it Ossie, maybe you should leave.'

'Okay Geoff, I'll play in the reserves on Wednesday as planned and then I'll collect my cards.'

As I walked out the door he muttered 'Yeah, yeah, I've heard it all before,' and I had to grit my teeth and stop myself turning around, launching across the table and whacking him.

Ossie had everything. He was as good in the air as he was on the ball. Peter could be a bit lazy, but he linked up with the midfield so well. He was a joy to play with and he both scored and made a hell of a lot of goals.

I. Hutchinson, Footballer

13

Last Orders

HUTCH WAS ALREADY FINISHED IN THE GAME. THE TERRIBLE TOLL OF THE injuries he had endured had forced him into early retirement. I played in his testimonial in November 1978, but he had not played a competitive match for a couple of years by then. Sadly, the game against Queens Park Rangers drew only a 4,000 crowd. A few of the lads got their testimonials around that time but it was a bad patch to be having them, as crowds were at a relatively low ebb for Chelsea. I was not the only one to have a second stint at Chelsea either. Alan Hudson came back, so did Charlie Cooke and John Hollins. It was as if there was unfinished business, for us and for the fans. We were like old men coming back to the family to live out their final years and die. Of the three of us, Charlie probably had the best second coming. History really did repeat itself in Huddy's case, for he left Chelsea for Stoke for a second time and remarkably helped them to stave off relegation yet again. I wished I'd had my synergy bet on that one. Professionally, I shouldn't have gone back. Chelsea had seen my finest days and I was now a shadow of the player I once was, only able to offer the Chelsea faithful the most fleeting of glimpses of that golden age. Emotionally, though, I was unable to say no.

With hindsight, something I have never had the foresight to acquire, I should have bitten my lip and carried on playing in the reserves instead of forcing the situation with Geoff. Perhaps I could have kept my head down and taken the reserves over. Maybe I would have ridden out Geoff's spell at the club (he didn't last too much longer either), gained valuable experience in coaching and stayed in the game. I would have liked nothing better than to have become part of Chelsea's backroom operation and see what developed from there. But it was not to be. I did play in that final reserve game, against Oxford United and in front of a couple of hundred people. Chopper was in the side and at the end of the game I cuddled him and said, 'See you Ron.'

'Yeah, see you Os.'

By the start of the following season, 1980–81, Geoff had let him go too. The only surviving member of our early '70s side. Last man standing. If anyone was going to go the distance it was always going to be Ronald Chopper Buller Harris.

In September 1979, then, I found myself unemployed but more importantly bereft. Since I was a boy of 15 football had been my life, each day of that life planned out for me. I never had to think 'What shall I do today?' or 'How will I pay this bill?' or 'Can I afford this?' I had stepped onto a ride as a boy clutching a shopping bag with some togs in it and had now been bundled off as a man on the cusp of middle age with few skills to cope with the real world. I was no different from other young men when it all started. Responsibility was a four-letter word (I never could add up), the future was so far away it didn't matter, and who cared anyway, everyone loved me. The difference is that most wild young men are faced with the reality of life a lot sooner than I was. They break free from the shield of their parents and take on the responsibilities of family and working life for themselves. Cold reality creeps in as they realise they are no different after all, and they mature and calm down. The clubs and managers were my parents, and while they were around I suppose I felt no need to mature. You could say that my teens lasted well into my 30s.

One of the biggest shocks was how quickly I became yesterday's man. Once you are out of the game, it appears, you almost become a non-person. Even though your name may figure in the record books, your face still instantly recognisable, you become almost irrelevant. The phone stops ringing, the invitations dry up and some of the friends who have been almost glued to your side ever since you can remember wander away looking sheepish. You see them again a few years later swilling lager and chortling as they stand around Kerry Dixon or whichever star is shining brightest at the time. I had seen enough ex-footballing heroes in reduced circumstances during my career, or politely reminding someone at their old club who they used to be, to know that this happened but I was not prepared for the speed of it. And, naturally, I never thought it would happen to me. I was the King of Stamford Bridge, remember?

But I was luckier than some, and did emerge from the game with some capital. Even I could not spend all the money as fast as I earned it, contrary to popular opinion. I felt I had to do something with it and immediately began looking for opportunities for investment in order to secure my future financially. Too many of my footballing colleagues had put their money into other people's ventures, never to see a penny back, so I was determined not to fall for any of these get-rich-quick schemes. Look at Webby, he had tried punting on almost everything with very little return except experience and some fun along the way. I decided that when I invested my money it would be best to remain close to it, and that it was paramount I get into something I knew about, preferably something I enjoyed. Therefore it didn't take long for me to reach the conclusion that I should buy a pub.

The Union Inn in Windsor was not an establishment I ever used. It had a reputation as a bit of a spit-and-sawdust dive, but it was a big gaff backing on to Crown land. When someone mentioned to me it was for sale I drove over there to have a look. On opening the door I could smell the stale urine wafting up from the old men's trousers, the seats were threadbare, the toilets were a shit-hole and the customers were conspicuous by their absence. A nice old gent had the place and we talked about the pub. The barrelage wasn't good, but it was a free house and I could see potential. 'How much do you want?' I asked.

'Eighty thousand.'

'Seventy.'

'As I knew your old dad. Done!' he spat into the palm of his hand and slapped it into mine, and I walked out of there wiping my hand on my trousers and as a publican-in-waiting.

I couldn't believe what I had just done. Firstly spending what was then a sizeable chunk of money (certainly a sizeable chunk of *my* money), and secondly committing myself to turning around what even I could see through my rose-coloured spectacles was an ailing business. And actually, I didn't know anything about running a pub at all, my experience being on the other side of the bar. But I was so excited that I had done the deed and now had something to occupy my empty days and work for that I had to tell people. One of those people was Hutch.

'Guess what I've just done?'

'Signed for Manchester United?' Hutch replied sarcastically.

'No, I've just bought a pub.'

'You're joking? You lucky bastard. That's what I want to do.'

I thought about what he'd said for about three seconds.

'Well, come in with me then.'

'Let me come and have a look,' he returned with uncharacteristic caution. I arranged to meet him in The Bells of Ouseley, a posh pub nearby that he knew how to get to. I had a lager on the bar waiting for him when he arrived. He picked up his pint, looked around the tastefully decorated bar and over towards the restaurant area and grinned. 'Yeah, this is the business Os, count me in.'

'No, no Hutch. This isn't the pub. Come with me.'

And so began the second incarnation of the famous Ossie and Hutch partnership.

It was what we both needed. We set about building the business up with gusto. Pippa and I were having a good patch, so we got married and Pippa and Hutch's girlfriend joined us in grafting away to make something of the place. If we thought the purchase price was the full extent of our large cash layouts we were very much mistaken. Refurbishing a big pub is a massive undertaking and we just had no real idea of the cost of such things, but we both had cash (although the Union was gulping it down) and our credit was still good. Eventually the place was finished and it now boasted a good restaurant and luxury bars. Hutch assumed responsibility for the food and I managed the drink. Very nicely, thank you. Actually, we both kept very sober most of the time. It's amazing how you like to keep your wits about you when your entire fortune, big or small, is up in the air. We attracted good chefs and bar staff and because we were still relatively famous we had little trouble in attracting the punters.

The Union Inn became something of an in-place to visit. Coaches returning from football matches often turned up, whether they were Chelsea or not, and local people came in large numbers, as well as curious people from much further afield. There was always a celebrity or two knocking about and although we sort of forgot it, Hutch and I were still a pull. Many a time a strange face would arrive, buy a drink, and then just sit and stare at me or Hutch busying ourselves around the place. Sometimes they'd strike up a conversation but other times they'd avoid eye contact, finish their drink and set off again. Jim Davidson was a regular, often dropping in for a drink before a gig.

Those were the days when he still boozed and a pre-performance slug seemed to calm him down. Elton John was a neighbour and another occasional visitor. Most of the lads from football visited regularly and it soon became as popular with some as Alexandres.

Donovan, for a short time England's reply to Bob Dylan, also used the pub occasionally and he asked us once if he could book the place for his son's 18th birthday. Hutch took the booking and began scribbling down the food requirements.

'What's your second name?' he enquired of Donovan as he left, as if he needed it for his paperwork. Donovan had said that we and our immediate crowd were welcome to join in the celebrations, but we took liberties and told every Tom, Dick and Harry. The party went on to four in the morning and me, Hutch and some of the lads were up on the tables singing and roaring. 'Here, Donovan,' I shouted as he passed me on the way to the toilet, 'sing us 'Mellow Yellow' will you?'

'I've done it three times already, Ossie!' he complained. But he got up and did it one more time.

We were both immensely pleased and proud that we had made it work. The money was coming in and even after paying all the expenses there was plenty left for us. On a good week 12 grand was passing through our tills. So this was what is meant by an investment. It was paying off already and the satisfaction of achieving something outside of football with no real outside help was great. However, I couldn't help feeling that it all seemed too easy. Whilst we were good grafters, me, Hutch and the girls, and even better socialisers, none of us were businessmen and we didn't have the sense to get someone in to look after our financial affairs or think ahead for us. It's a familiar story, and one that some will find hard to believe, but although we had vague knowledge of a responsibility to conserve cash for taxes and suchlike, because it was something we had never dealt with personally we left it to the tax fairy to sort out.

Hutch never played football for his country, but he could shag for England. He had a way with women; I think they wanted to mother him. Some of his conquests were older than my mother. He got himself into a spot of bother once with a young lady who used to come to the pub to empty our fruit machines. He struck up a relationship with her and before I knew it, the ritual of emptying the machines seemed to be taking a lot longer than it should and I had to make myself scarce when the lady was around. We became friends with her too, and were not surprised when she told us that her and her husband (yes, she was married) had got the lease on a nice little pub in Surrey and we wouldn't be seeing her anymore. Hutch obviously did though, for a year or so later he had the shock of his life when he was pulled in by the police to 'help with the investigation of a murder'. He was held for eight hours and only worked out why when they continually enquired about various belts that he may have worn. It transpired that the lady's unfortunate husband had been strangled with a belt in the garden of his home and the police were pursuing the line of enquiry that a jealous lover of the lady had carried out the killing. Fortunately for Hutch, he was just one of many that fitted into the 'lover' category and he had a solid alibi for the night in question. He was with me. The murder became front-page news and the true story was unravelled fairly quickly. The landlady, as she now was, had struck up a relationship with a young soldier and between them they cooked up a plan to dispose of the unwanted husband. The soldier was charged, tried and imprisoned, as was Hutch's former lady friend. The pub in Surrey has been known by the affectionate nickname of 'The Stranglers' ever since.

Hutch had a thing going with the draymen. I'm not trying to pretend I knew nothing about it – I did, but I had not personally arranged it and frankly took little notice of it. I guess it was a bit of an illegal perk for the draymen; I can't imagine we were the only publicans that they had this arrangement with. It went like this: they delivered bottled soft drinks but gave us more than was on the receipt, which basically meant that we were getting a small proportion of our soft drinks for free each week and the draymen were getting a 'drink' (some cash) from us. This went on for as long as I can remember, and Hutch and I put it down to one of the many slightly shady practices that seemed to go on in this industry we had found ourselves in.

One morning the police raided the pub. They were from Aldershot. I knew they wouldn't be local police, as we enjoyed good relations with them and many of their senior officers used the Union Inn regularly, especially for late drinks. I had absolutely no idea what it was all about. Maybe Hutch had got involved with another murderess? They crawled all over the place. The one in charge asked me to produce the receipts for the soft drinks delivered by the draymen. The penny started dropping. They took me round the back of the pub and confronted me with the empty crates. After cautioning me, they asked, 'How can you explain that there are significantly more crates here than are detailed on the receipts?'

'They must be fucking breeding,' I suggested.

The police did not see the funny side and seemed to be taking the whole business alarmingly seriously. They carted us off to Aldershot nick where they proceeded to separate us and subject each of us to detailed interrogation. They even tried the age-old trick of saying to me that Hutch had spilled the beans, and claimed it was all down to me. I know we were hardly Reggie and Ronnie but there was no way either of us would fall for that old chestnut. They then threw us in the cells for eight hours to stew over it.

Eventually Hutch and I were charged with defrauding the brewery and committed to trial at Winchester Crown Court. Whatever next? When the day came for the trial we were both nervous. Our lawyers had explained that by pleading 'not guilty' and electing to be tried in Crown Court we had raised the stakes considerably. The Crown Court had higher sentencing powers than a magistrates court, and prison could be an option should we be found guilty. Our relative celebrity status, they explained, could work for us but it could also work against us. Our defence was based on the fact that we didn't really know what was going on; whilst we realised that the arrangement was irregular we did not know it was criminal.

I knew we were walking free as soon as we stood in the dock and looked over the rail at the jury. Some openly smiled at us and others had a twinkle in their eye. As the trial progressed a picture emerged of me and Hutch as some sort of Laurel and Hardy partnership bumbling our way through the world of business, but the jury were won over completely when counsel cross-examined the police officer. 'How did Mr Osgood explain the discrepancy between the number of crates in storage and those that had receipts?'

'Mr Osgood said the crates must be fucking breeding, sir.'

The whole place erupted into laughter, much to the annoyance of the judge, but after that there was no way this jury was going to convict us. And they didn't. After we left a man ran up to us, all smiles. 'All right Ossie, all right Hutch. I'm Chelsea me. Through and through. You two were guilty as fuck but us Chelsea boys got to stick together. Right?'

'Who was that?' asked Hutch. 'I recognise him from somewhere.'

'You should do, Hutch, you've been looking straight at him for the last few days. He was one of the jury, you berk!'

I don't remember the name of the man from Customs & Excise but I can remember his face clearly. He looked like the weasel he was and turned up one day with a young lady carrying his bags. 'I'm here to do the VAT inspection,' he announced.

'Go ahead,' I said.

'I need to see your books.'

Problem number one. I would have liked to have seen our books. Our record keeping was erratic to say the least. The more he saw, or more accurately the less he saw, the more annoyed he became. He started to tell me off like I was a naughty kid.

'Look mate, just tell us what we owe, how you want us to keep records and we'll do it, no point in keeping going on.'

'We'll be in touch,' he grunted and swept out of the pub.

Get in touch they did, courtesy of a brown envelope that demanded £30,000 within 30 days. I rang them up, 'Thirty thousand quid! You're having a laugh. How can we owe that? You might as well ask for 300,000 quid.'

But they were not up for negotiating. Totally inflexible, they started talking about distraint orders, disqualification and so on. I just smashed the phone down. Hutch and I talked it over and began to rack our brains on how to raise the money. We didn't want to let the pub go, as we knew it was inherently profitable. But at the same time our relationship was beginning to come under strain.

Hutch's girlfriend at the time worked in the City and was obviously bringing in a salary for the two of them. Pippa was my wife and she was working in the pub full time, yet she was not taking a salary out of the business. Pippa and I felt this was unfair but when we raised it with Hutch he could not see our side of the argument at all. We started shouting at one another, as we sometimes did, but this time my goat was really up. I backed him into the kitchens and whilst we screamed at one another a microwave oven beeped. I instinctively turned around and switched it off.

'Don't touch my equipment,' Hutch said.

'What d'you mean, your equipment?'

'The kitchen and restaurant is my area, get back in the bar.'

At that the red mist descended and I leapt forward and cracked him as hard as I could with my fist, and he flew backwards into the saucepans and the arms of the frightened kitchen staff. I immediately regretted it. Hutch was my best mate. I loved him. He was best man at my second wedding. He looked after me on the pitch. He's had terrible luck and he didn't deserve that. But all of a sudden everything seemed to be going wrong around us and like an old married couple we blamed each other and started to take it out on one another.

The following morning we sheepishly talked. Hutch had a black eye and I apologised again.

'I never thought you'd do that to me, bruv,' he muttered quietly as he stared down at the floor. That made me feel worse.

'Let's go outside now, Hutch, and you can give me a smack and then we're quits,' I offered in desperation.

'No Os, it's too late.' We decided we had to call it a day. The trial had been an ordeal, our personal relationship had suffered to the point we were now coming to blows and the debt to the tax man seemed insurmountable. Regrettably we gave up rather than learn from our mistakes. We declared ourselves bankrupt and put the pub on to the market.

Pippa also decided to jump the sinking ship around this time. The relationship was always volatile, but towards the end we became very distant. I suspected she was seeing someone else but didn't care, which sort of summed up how bad things had become. She took what belongings I had left and the realisation hit me that I was nearly 40 years of age yet my entire assets could be carried around with me in an Adidas bag.

Some time later Dad died. He had been ill for some years and his last months were particularly torrid. He was a great man and a wonderful dad to us and a good husband to Mum. He had always been there, the same old steady Dad, and when he went it was such a shock even though we had all known it was coming. After the funeral I got back to the old house before everyone else and just sat down. It seemed so empty without him and all the memories danced around in front of me. I put on his favourite Perry Como LP and let the ancient gramophone play it over and over. I heard his voice and his laugh in my head, looked over at his chair, trying to get my head around the fact that I would never see, hear or touch him again. Not in this life anyway. The tears literally burst out of me and I cried more than I have ever cried before, or ever have since.

Peter . . . who?
S. G. Eriksson, Football Manager

14

Up Pompey

I HAD REACHED MY LOWEST EBB. I WAS BANKRUPT AND HAD LOST TWO WIVES, my dear dad and my two boys. Lost the plot. Very careless. I was even living back at Mum's or kindly being put up by friends, especially Dougie and Karen, who cared for me when I was at rock bottom. I began to feel like the wastrel plenty of people had told me over the years I was. 'Ossie, you wasted your talent.' 'Ossie, you waste your money.' 'Ossie, you'll come a cropper one day.' Those annoying words had now come back to haunt me. I hated to admit it, because at the time if anyone told me anything I wilfully ignored it – I knew best, but maybe they were right? None of the other lads seemed to have fallen on hard times as spectacularly or as rapidly as Hutch and myself. By contrast Ronnie Harris had graduated from sweet shops to golf courses and had become a millionaire by selling his land to the golf-hungry Japanese. Some of the other lads were still hanging on in the game in one capacity or another. Johnny Hollins had slipped into the manager's seat at Chelsea; Eddie and Charlie were making lives for themselves out in the States; Peter Bonetti was coaching the goalkeepers down at the Bridge; Dave Sexton had been manager at Manchester United and was now part of the England set-up; and Huddy was living up in Stoke, where he remained a local hero.

This was a watershed point in my life and fortunately for me I recognised it. I could carry on downward and eventually become an old pisshead, swapping a story or two in the pub for a drink, or I could stop feeling sorry for myself, pick myself up and fight back. I was still

young (old for a footballer but young for most other things), had my
health and, as always, enjoyed life. Things could have been much,
much worse. I started work with a pal as a painter and decorator. My
face was still fairly recognisable at the time, my footballing career not
having ended that long before, so it caused some double-takes now
and then when I turned up at a customer's house in my overalls with
my brush and paint.

Then I had my luckiest break. I was driving to the bank to pay
some money in when I saw Lynn, a former girlfriend who worked for
the world's favourite airline, BA, in a ground staff role. We had first
met at the Mile High Club for British Airways staff some time before.
We stopped and chatted. I told her that my marriage with Pippa was
over and discovered that she was not currently in a relationship
either. The feelings we'd had for one another quickly rekindled. We
began courting again and took it slowly and cautiously, but within a
few months I left Mum's and moved into Lynn's place. She was a
great influence on me, giving me love and boosting my self-
confidence no end. Being in a secure, loving relationship again was a
revelation and suddenly my financial and career problems seemed
insignificant.

One of the wonderful things about being part of the football
industry is the great camaraderie that exists between the people in it.
In all my years in the game, I can honestly say that the amount of
people I came across that I genuinely disliked I could count on the
thumbs of one hand. In my time at least it was populated by nice,
warm, and often very funny people. As this book has recorded, I fell
out with a few bods along the way, but that's life. I have no bitterness
and can't recall ever feeling any ill will to anyone for more than a few
days. I think we are all really bound together by the sheer insecurity of
it. The knowledge that you can be up there one minute and down the
bottom the next. That good teams are only really together for the
shortest of times. That you are only as good as your last few games at
any given time. Only a few of us ever made the mistake of believing
our own publicity. One day someone could be your team mate, the
next he could be your manager. The manager also knew that one day
he could be on the dole and looking to you for a favour, and so on.
So when your luck is in you attempt to look after as many of your pals
as you safely can. You often see it when managers move clubs and take
their assistants with them. It is debatable whether the assistant is
necessarily the best person for the job, or indeed if there really is a

need for an assistant manager at all. Nine times out of ten it is the boys looking after each other.

On a smaller scale, Alan Ball was looking after me when he rang me up to tell me he had been appointed youth team manager of Portsmouth Football Club in the mid '80s. 'Well done, Bally!' I congratulated him.

'The point is Ossie, do you want my old job?'

Bally had been working for Butlins coaching holidaymakers' kids. It involved driving around the country to the various camps and holding coaching sessions in each one. The job was reasonably well paid and came with a car. For me it was a no-brainer. I would be doing something I liked, something I thought I could be good at and most importantly, in the smallest of ways, I would be back involved in the game I love.

And I did love it. The kids really got something out of it, even though the sessions were only for a couple of hours. The thrill of having an ex-England international giving them one-to-one coaching seemed to make their holiday. Most of them knew who I was, as well as the other lads on the circuit, like Paul Reaney, the former Leeds full-back, but their dads seemed even more taken with it. I got the impression that these men in their 20s, 30s and 40s would have preferred to have swatted their kids aside and coached with us instead. The work was arduous, though, as most of my time was spent on the road. I'd take a session in the morning in, say, Bognor Regis in Sussex and then jump into the car to make a late afternoon session in Minehead, Somerset, and then the next day head up country to Tenby and so on. Very often I'd flop into bed in one of the empty apartments exhausted and falling asleep to the excited chatter of the holidaymakers as they passed the chalet outside on their way for a mammoth night of drinking and partying in one of the ballrooms. A few years before I'd have been out joining them on the razzle whether I knew anyone or not. I must have been getting old.

The realisation that I was ageing was reinforced when I bumped into the parade of old pop stars who were now making their living from the holiday camp circuit. The parallels with us old footballers did not go unnoticed but at least we were not forced to exist in some sort of ghoulish time bubble. They were expected to look like they did in their heyday but personally I found the groups of 50-year-old men with long hair, middle-aged spreads jammed into sequin suits and more chins than a Peking phone book gruesome. They were all there at one time or other: The Troggs, Billy J. Kramer, The Merseybeats, Herman's Hermits (but strangely with no Herman), The Fortunes et al.

As I ate breakfast one morning I couldn't help but stare at the apparition sitting opposite me. His face was drawn and only the toilet seats of a London nightclub on a Saturday night could have had more lines on it. The face was framed by the most garish peroxide hair and he steadied his trembling hand with his other not-so-trembling one as he tried to raise a glass of orange juice to his lips. There was no doubt – it was Brian Connolly, lead singer of The Sweet, heart-throb to millions of teenagers only some 15 years previously. Someone told me later that he was the brother of Mark McManus, who played Taggart on the TV, and looking back I can believe it. Imagine Taggart in a blonde Dusty Springfield wig and you'll get a picture of what Brian Connolly looked like that morning.

When it rained and I couldn't hold the coaching session we'd duck indoors into the ballroom, our shoes sticking to the carpet, still soaked in last night's spilt beer, and sit around a table where I would conduct little question-and-answer sessions. Some of the boys wanted to talk tactics, but more often than not they would ask me about my career with Chelsea, Southampton and England. Particularly they wanted to hear the funny stories. What was Chopper Harris really like? Did I really play with a hip flask full of brandy in my shorts? Who nicked the bracelet in Mexico? The dads would shuffle over and before I knew it I was playing to an audience on these occasions. I noticed the questions were pretty much the same ones nearly every time and I soon evolved a patter. One day I was approached by a man I had never met. 'Have you thought about going on the after-dinner circuit?' he asked.

'Oh, I couldn't do that.' I shook my head. 'Get up in front of all those people and talk like that.'

'That's exactly what you're doing here and you've got some great stories. I think you're a natural.' He handed me his card.

Much as I loved the job, it was wearing me down. The constant treadmill of driving from one seaside town to another was draining me and I started to resent the time I had to spend away from Lynn. Sometimes she managed to join me at one of the camps, but we were spending far too much time apart for my liking. I did not want this relationship to go the way of the others and knew only too well the perils of leading separate lives. 'Absence makes the heart grow fonder' may be applicable for small periods of time apart, but sustained estrangements can only lead to 'out of sight, out of mind'.

We married in Waltham Chase, Hampshire in 1987. We hired a Rolls Royce for the wedding and as we sat in it together waiting, because we were a bit ahead of schedule Lynn suggested we visit the pub and have a drink. I knew then that this lady was going to make me very, very happy. My two boys came and I joked with Anthony, the eldest, 'How does it feel to have been at all three of your old man's weddings?' He was at my first, remember, if only in embryonic form.

Just when Lynn and I were sitting down to consider my career options the phone rang. It was that voice again. Alan Ball. 'Alright, Ossie, how do you fancy joining me here at Portsmouth.'

'Love to, Boss. Doing what?'

'Youth team coach.'

Alan was doing well at Portsmouth, and was now the first team manager. They had just come out of the old Third Division and were becoming a solid Second Division side with their sights set firmly on the First Division, which would soon become the Premiership. Bally had taken the club by the scruff of the neck and was laying down the foundations for the future. He told me what he wanted from me.

'There's no money here for players Os, but there is plenty of talent around. I want you to help find the youngsters, but more importantly I want you to develop them and when you think they're ready give me the nod.'

It meant a slight drop in wages but that didn't matter; I loved working with the kids. Spotting talent and where possible developing it. I did it to a small extent on the holiday camps but to be part of a club again, and a team, was a dream come true. I knew that Bally was in it for real and that, like on the field, he'd be a dynamo. If he didn't succeed it wouldn't be for want of trying. Graham Paddon, the former Norwich and West Ham player who had also worked the camps, was reserve team manager and we got on great too. I couldn't wait to be let off the leash.

Over the years I had formed my own thoughts and ideas about tactics, coaching and management that I would have loved to have put into practice and at Portsmouth I got the chance to do just that. I am a great believer in the old 4-2-4 system when you are attacking, and dropping back to 4-4-2 when you are defending. You can't beat wingers playing out wide and getting behind defenders. They don't like it behind 'em. Defenders don't like crosses. It's all pretty simple stuff, but at various periods football has gone up its own backside and tried to be too clever. I hear people say on the TV about someone being 'a great technical player' – what on earth does that really mean? 'Director of Football'. What's all that about? I was fortunate enough to have played under three great, down-to-earth managers – Tommy Docherty, Dave Sexton and Lawrie McMenemy, and if a person came along that combined the qualities of those three then we'd have the greatest manager of all time. Docherty's raw enthusiasm and nose for spotting talent, Sexton's coaching brilliance and McMenemy's motivational and organisational skills, along with his intellect, would have been unbeatable.

I worry a bit about the game I love. Where are the 20-a-side park matches with rush goalies I used to play in as a boy? How often do you see kids playing football in the streets? Where are the next lot of English footballers coming from? And you don't have to be a genius to work out that things in the professional game are on the brink of changing radically. Just like an over-inflated stock market, a correction is due. The majority of clubs were only just about holding their heads above water before satellite or digital television money was reduced. And as every ordinary person knows, more money out than money in ends in tears. Very soon running costs will have to be cut so that they do not exceed receipts. In the past losses could be sustained by the largesse of the chairman and directors – but there is a big difference between paying for a new clubhouse and personally guaranteeing a £20m overdraft. Businessmen who are willing and able to do this are few and far between. Inevitably, many of the bigger name players will seek satisfaction of their financial goals elsewhere. More and more clubs will have to look again to their local communities as the key source of their revenue, and with the reduction of foreign players in Britain more local lads will eventually play in the higher divisions. Some current Second and Third Division clubs may find themselves using a pool of amateur players. Bricklayers in the week and centre-forwards at the weekend. But as long as the path of progression from amateur leagues to Premiership is not closed off, I believe the game will survive beyond a yearly, sparkling televised super-club special. For it is the spectacle of seeing a Wimbledon, Wycombe or Rushden come from nowhere to scale the heights that makes English League football so delicious.

One idea I had which I believe would help reinvigorate the

country's interest in the domestic game and help bind football at all levels together, as well as generating much needed revenues, is for a competition called The British County Cup. It could be played every four years in the close season and each British county would be able to enter. Only players who were born in the county could play and the manager of the county side for the tournament would also have to be born in that county. There would be no 'my auntie went on holiday to Cornwall once so I qualify for Cornwall' lark. It would be a simple knock-out ending in a final at a neutral ground. I believe it would generate huge interest and bring out good-natured 'nationalistic' rivalry among the counties and draw in new fans. It would also be a marvellous showcase for new players, with the likes of David Beckham, for instance, playing alongside Bill Perkins, star centre-forward of Bookham Cherrypickers.

The Bosman rule has a lot to answer for. Why should clubs be expected to invest huge amounts of money in player wages when the player can simply walk away on a free transfer at the end of a period? It does not make sense. The emergence of agents hasn't helped either. The days of exploitative chairman and clubs were almost over when I was a player, so the need for agents to negotiate players' contracts is questionable. Their presence has only served to widen the gap between fans, players and clubs. If fans, players and clubs do not feel connected then the fabric that has made football what it has been for a century will fall away.

On my first day at Pompey Alan took me to meet the first team squad. 'This is Peter Osgood. Now this man could *really* play football. He's joining us as youth team coach.' Then, eyeballing Noel Blake, a very well-built boy, he added, 'He also likes a fight.' Thanks Bally. He said much the same to the youth players but urged them to look and learn. These were the 14–16 year olds and it was my job to mould and coach them, and then decide who would be retained and who would be let go. There was a talented pool of players, including Mark Kelly, Kit Simons, Liam Daish, Darryl Powell and Paul Musselwhite. It came to decision time with one lad, a small mousy-haired boy who I felt had great talent but was just too weak to make it in the professional game. 'It's a tough call Gaffer, but I think we'll have to let him go,' I said. Bally and Graham Paddon both felt we should persevere with him though, and in the end we did. Good job too, as the boy was the future Tottenham and England international Darren Anderton. Darren has sadly been plagued by injury in his career, to the point where some sections of supporters have cruelly nicknamed him 'Sicknote'.

Liam Daish was a big local lad who hailed from one of the rougher parts of town and apparently he had a reputation at first for being something of handful. One of the first things Bally said to me was 'See the big fella, that's Daishey. Get rid.'

The gaffer had decided that his influence was too overbearing and that his presence might be impeding some of the quieter boys' progress. I took on board what he told me but on watching Liam I could see he was a very useful young player. One morning I asked him to see me in the gym after training. When he turned up I could see he was tense and ready for a row.

'Daishey,' I said, 'I hear you like a bit of a fight.' He eyed me menacingly, probably pondering on which part of my jaw to break. 'Well, do you want to fight me or do you want to be my captain?'

His demeanour softened. 'You serious?'

'Course I'm serious.' I went to the gaffer and told him I was not going to let the boy go and felt I could build the team around him. Bally was not impressed and said it was against his better judgement, but that he had promised me the reins and the result of the decision would be on my head. Unlike with young Darren I was proved right on this one; Daishey became the linchpin of the side and went on to have a good professional career.

It took a while for the players to gel under me and after one game against Tottenham where we lost 10–0, I offered my resignation. 'Shut up,' said Alan. 'I don't care about leagues. You just bring me good players, Ossie, that's what you're here for.'

After that I relaxed a bit. It reminded me of when Tommy Doc pledged me those ten consecutive first team appearances all those years ago. The team did get better as various individuals flowered and after winning a game in the semi-final of an important cup for the youth sides, I was delighted.

'The gaffer will be in in a second, I'm not going to say anything until then,' I told them as they sat around grinning and congratulating one another. They had all played out of their skins.

Bally bustled in. 'Well done lads,' he started, 'but I'm sorry, you'll have no chance against Watford in the final. They are a different class. You might as well not turn up.' And he turned and left the changing-rooms. I couldn't believe it – they were kids, after all, and they'd just won the biggest game of their careers so far.

'Don't take any notice of that,' I pleaded. 'He don't know what he's talking about.' But the gaffer is the gaffer and it deflated them completely.

We went to Watford and the lads played beyond their ability. They nicked an early lead and against all the odds and severe pressure held it. Portsmouth were 1–0 winners and the boys had played their best football so far. For me, it was one of the most rewarding matches I have never played in and one of the highs of my entire life. The boss and the first team were away on tour but I made a point of ringing the hotel when I knew Bally would be in bed. '1–0,' I said when he finally answered. Then I put the phone down.

I don't know whether he was asleep or watching the erotic movie, but I'm sure a self-satisfied smile would have crept across his face as he congratulated himself on his clever little mind games with me and the boys working out again.

The set-up at Fratton Park was great. Besides Alan and Graham running the first and reserve team respectively, we had Dave Hurst, who had been scouting at the club since the days when the Isle of Wight was still attached to the mainland. Dave would industriously scour the area for players and when someone took his fancy get me down to take a look. Bobby Stokes, my old mate from Southampton and scorer of one of Wembley's more famous goals, was also helping out, as was John Harris who did sterling work in keeping the whole thing on the road as youth team sponsor. In the 1986–87 season the club won promotion to the First Division (Premiership) for the first time in many years.

I felt personally involved with all the players – the ones that went on to bigger and better things and the ones that didn't. We were a real family and therefore when I had the job of telling boys they were not going to make it, it hurt me almost as much as it hurt them. Normally this involved tears. One lad, Lee Darby, cried when I told him we *were* taking him on as a pro. There was another boy called John Cox. He was one of the most decent kids I ever worked with and I remember once being furious when a big first team player called Micky Kennedy smacked him in training. I knew John wasn't going to make it so I spoke to his parents and told them first.

'John is getting better all the time,' I explained, 'but I honestly believe he does not have the complete make-up needed to become a professional player. We will have to let him go. But John is a smashing kid and everyone here loves having him around, so if he wants to see the year out with us, he'd be more than welcome.'

John took the news very well and was delighted to stay with us for the rest of the year, despite knowing that there was no career at the end of it.

Not all the parents were as pragmatic. There was a boy called Lee Russell who I felt didn't go the extra mile (pot calling kettle black?) and I gave him untold stick from the touchline. His mother didn't take too kindly to this and admonished me once in public. 'Why do you keep picking on my boy? What about the others?'

'Mrs Russell, if you don't like it your Lee can pack his bags and leave Portsmouth Football Club this afternoon.'

Lee must have been mortified that his mum had dug me out, if he knew about it, but when the day came to tell him that he was being taken on professionally he thanked me for giving him a hard time. To her credit his mum came to see me too, apologised and thanked me for driving her boy.

None of us were completely shattered when Portsmouth slipped back down to the Second Division. Then, as now, it was a struggle to stay in the top flight without serious injections of funds and we felt that the fundamentals were right and this was a hiccough rather than a permanent set-back. I had been awarded a three-year contract on the condition that I committed myself to the club more by moving my home closer to Fratton Park. It was a big decision that involved Lynn selling her place where we were living and uprooting away from her family and network of friends. But we decided we should demonstrate our commitment even though we knew that the way house prices were moving it would be hard to ever move back towards London. Therefore I felt stable and did not become too alarmed when chairman John Deacon (whose health had been failing for some time) decided he'd had enough and sold the club to Jim Gregory.

I felt for Bally when he called me in to see him one afternoon after training. He didn't beat around the bush. 'The chairman has told me to fire you.'

'What?' I was literally dumbstruck. Things were going so well. I was happy, and I knew Bally was happy. Portsmouth's youth team set-up was already paying dividends and the club were enjoying their best years for some time. Also I had two years left on my contract. Most importantly, though, Lynn and I had not long sold our house and bought one locally. Bally told me that the official reason was cost-cutting, but that Jim Gregory was a good friend of Dave Sexton, and we also knew maybe he was getting some sort of weird, belated revenge for the wrongs he believed that I had committed on Dave. I didn't like the synergy in that one. Poor old Alan, he had no choice in the matter. He was not going to go out on a limb because of me and I wouldn't expect him to. We both knew the game only too well. He might be next. (He was.)

I went to see Jim myself. He had a bit of a reputation as a hard-nosed chairman. The Doc had warned me about him, having fallen foul of him at Queens Park Rangers, but I was hoping he might see reason when I got in front of him.

'What goes round, comes round,' he repeated a couple of times in our conversation.

'What do you mean by that?' I demanded.

He wouldn't elaborate, but I knew what he meant all right. He stuck to the 'times are hard' story. 'I'll give you three months' money but you must collect your stuff and leave today.'

'I'm sorry, Mr Gregory, but I have two years left on my contract. You'll have to honour that.'

'Will I?' he laughed sarcastically. 'This is my club. I own it and I'll do what I want. Now run along Osgood, and take your three months' pay before I change my mind and give you fuck-all.'

I was crushed to lose my job, just at a time when I was getting more satisfaction than at almost any other time in my career, and I knew I was really contributing something worthwhile. But I understood the see-saw nature of employment in this industry. I would live with it, but I was angry at being treated so shabbily by Gregory. Even if the real reason *was* cost-cutting he expressed no regret at having to let me go. He was smarmy and rude. Therefore I can only draw the conclusion that his real motive was loyalty to his friend Dave Sexton. The spat with Dave had occurred nearly 15 years earlier and had nothing to do with Jim Gregory whatsoever. Had he treated me fairly I would have compromised. It happened I took him to an industrial tribunal, something I never thought I'd do in a million years. Times had changed since the days when employers could treat their staff with contempt, and without any recognition of employment law or fair play. Gregory believed that because he was powerful he could do exactly what he wanted. That's how he had always carried on, but the world was changing. For all of us.

As the day of the tribunal neared he contacted me to settle out of court. Suddenly he was calling me Ossie. Obviously his lawyers had told him what mine had told me – that he did not have a leg to stand on. But I was going to take him for what I could now and only at the last minute did I accept an offer that was pretty close to what I was owed. He did not like it at all. Even for a rich man it was a lot of cash to lay out when the minimum redundancy payment was one week for every year. When I saw him, I patted him on the back and whispered in his ear, 'What goes round, comes round.'

What can you say about Ossie? He's a fucking legend. I put him up there with Bestie, I really do. I loved playing with him, he had such a skill for a big fella and I think we complemented one another. He trained hard when I knew him so I don't have much track with that 'lazy Osgood' talk, but he also played hard. Loved a drink and a laugh. I remember one of his car crashes when one of the papers pictured his motor upside down in a field. One of the lads tore it out and put it on the wall in the changing-rooms. Where his number plate was visible PO9, I drew in pen a T between the P and the O. When he came in he asked what it meant. 'Please turn over' I said. He liked that did Ossie. Another time he turned up with odd shoes on and we ripped it out of him. 'I've got another pair like this at home,' he laughed. He's still got the same twinkle in his eye, even now, that he had when I first met him when I was a 17-year-old kid playing for Southampton against Chelsea.

M. Channon, Racecourse Trainer

15

Meeting, Greeting and Speaking

BY NOW I WAS GETTING USED TO GOING BACK TO SQUARE ONE. LYNN AND I had the arrival of our lovely young son, Darren, to take our minds off my lack of employment but I was determined to bounce back. There was no point in sitting at home wasting time wondering why 'Hi Ho Silver Lining' doesn't get played at weddings anymore or why so many of the Chelsea Cup-winning sides had surnames beginning with 'H'. This time I wanted something where I was not subject to the whims of rich men or a run of bad football results. I noticed that interest in my era of playing was at a peak and many of my old colleagues were carving out a living on the after-dinner circuit. I'd seen one or two in action and, as you do, thought 'I can do that'. I remembered what the man at the holiday camp had told me and although I no longer had his business card, I put myself down with an agency as an after-dinner speaker.

Without Lynn I would never have done it. She coaxed me, coached me, encouraged me and pushed me in the nicest possible way. Her close friend Elaine had attended drama school and she was friendly there with a great young guy called Roland. His ambition was to become a comedy scriptwriter. Lynn thought it would be a good idea if he wrote a script around the experiences I recounted to him. Roland kindly did this, and then Lynn and I spent hours in our front room practising and honing the act, with me standing at one end as the performer, and her sitting at the other as the audience. If any nosy neighbour had peered through the French windows they would have thought we had a real communication problem, as I stood at the other side of the room projecting my voice to her and she sat, arms folded, occasionally breaking into applause.

My first gig was at the School House in Manchester and as they say in footballing circles I had a 'mare. Never, ever have I suffered from such nerves. Old boys like Joe Royle and Mick Doyle were there and I literally died on my feet. I had butterflies in the old days, sometimes before a big match or if there was a lot at stake personally, but they were butterflies of anticipation. This was cold, horrible fear. When I stood up the sweat trickled down my back, my hands trembled and I read very amateurishly from a prompt sheet of paper. I contemplated running out of the building and cursed myself for getting myself into this position in the first place. My lines were not spontaneous, they were not funny and they were delivered quickly and without any feeling. Like a man who is in a hurry to get off stage, which is exactly what I was. Peter Brackley, the sports commentator, was the link man and when I finished he said, 'Thank you Peter Osgood, for 30 seconds of laughs and 30 minutes of I'm not sure what.'

That line got a better reception than my whole act.

I really was mortified. Peter approached me after and cheered me up a little. 'That was absolutely terrible, Ossie.' However, he also said there was nothing wrong with the material, that it was fresh and honest, but I had to learn how to structure it better, remember it and deliver it. Being spontaneous takes a lot of work I would learn. He said there was a charity golf weekend coming up and suggested I came along. There I would meet the comedian and singer Richard Digance, and Peter said he'd be glad to give me a few tips.

Lynn and I went to the golf do and I was introduced to Richard. What a smashing man! We sat by the swimming pool, and he switched on his tape machine and he endured my whole act. Only once did he wince. Never did he laugh.

'Give me a couple of hours, Ossie,' he smiled, then disappeared up to his room. I thought he might be going off to hang himself.

When he returned he handed me a script and a tape that he had done as if he was me. It was the same material, but he had transformed it by sharpening it up. He taught me about timing and delivery, and enjoying myself, and told me to go home and practise in front of a mirror until I was comfortable. He assured me it would come. The next time I appeared in front of an audience I still had a lot to learn, but I was better and the reaction from the audience was noticeably warmer. Thanks Richard.

He taught me that it was always best to open up with a joke or two before launching into 'My name is Peter Osgood and 30 years ago I was a young bricklayer working in Windsor . . !'

I remember the first couple he gave me: 'Bill Wyman is a great Chelsea fan, he was hoping to be here tonight but he has been called to the hospital to attend the birth of his next wife,' and 'George Best can't be here unfortunately. He was asked to launch a ship at the Harland & Wolff shipyard in Belfast but is now seven miles adrift in the Irish Sea after refusing to let go of the bottle.' It did get better.

The work started to roll in and I was again thoroughly enjoying myself. Lynn started to look after the business side of it all (no more Union Inn debacles, thank you), I just turned up. My work took me all over Britain and beyond. I could be in Dunstable one night and Dubai the next. I met more old pals on the circuit than I had since I retired from playing. Besty and Marsh were the market leaders, playing to packed houses all over. Retro TV programmes, videos and magazines were all the rage and the appetite for anything 1960s and '70s seemed unquenchable. I even considered relaunching my Peter Osgood football boots.

Once I had the misfortune to do a show with Rodney Marsh. He was fielding some questions when he was asked if he ever came across drugs in the game. 'Osgood's on next, you better ask him,' he quipped.

A quip it may have been, but I did not like it. I have never taken drugs in my life, never even smoked a fag, so it wasn't really funny and I told him so.

'Don't get out your pram,' he replied.

But he did it another time, so I warned him that if he ever used the joke again I'd smash his head open. On stage too. Haven't seen him since.

Meanwhile my local golf club, Meon Valley, had made me an honorary member and Lynn and I started organising golf weekends with the help of Terry Hussey, the then manager, which proved to be a great success and another string to the small but growing family enterprise. Again it was something we enjoyed immensely. But the icing on the cake was yet to come. Chelsea Football Club had finally emerged from the footballing doldrums. Bobby Campbell, the man Alan Ball had succeeded at Portsmouth, had steered them out of Division Two and David Webb had just had a period in charge as caretaker manager in the new Premiership. Ken Bates owned the club by then and the Mears family had faded away into the archives. Bates was controversial, abrasive, spoke his mind and didn't suffer fools gladly. His only drawback was that he was of the opinion that almost everyone else was a fool. But no one could deny he was presiding over a renaissance at Stamford Bridge and although Webby had performed well in the hot seat, Ken had his eyes on what he saw as bigger things and installed Glenn Hoddle, gifted player and darling of Tottenham Hotspur, as manager. The rest is history. Glenn spawned Ruud Gullit, Ruud spawned Gianluca Vialli and Gianfranco Zola and before we knew it the glory days had returned.

Webby, I believe, urged the chairman to get some of the old players down in a corporate hospitality capacity and I got a call from Ken Bates asking me if I would like to meet, greet and mix on match days. Okay, if you insist. I would have paid Chelsea to spend my Saturdays doing just that! It was wonderful to be back meeting the fans, old and new, the players and everyone else at the club. Ken's revolution was pulling the old and new together nicely and nurturing a real spirit of history and future. Whilst expensive foreign players were arriving, new bars were being built named after past players such as myself, Bobby Tambling and Roy Bentley. The buzz at the place was tangible. Alan Hudson too was back doing the same thing as me. He told me a funny story. Ken was showing him around the stadium as the redevelopment work was progressing. He swept his hands apart and pointed to the North Stand end. 'Down there we're going to have a bar called Tambling's.'

'That's nice,' acknowledged Alan.

'And over here I'm putting in a bar called Huddy's.'

Alan's chest swelled up. 'Thank you Ken, that's really touching.'

'Yeah, I've always been a massive Roy Hudd fan,' countered the chairman.

The job was hectic. I would arrive around midday and pop into the Imperial or another local pub to have a drink with the Chelsea boys. Some I knew, some I didn't. Many of these lads I would never come across in corporate hospitality and I didn't want to lose touch with the grass roots. That's what we used to do. Why change now? Then I would nip across to the ground. Often I was late due to stopping and signing autographs and exchanging a few words with people keen to talk to me. 'You're five minutes' late' I was sometimes told. What did they want me to do? Shun the fans and hurry into the club like some prima donna?

Once there I would show corporate sponsors around the club and the trophy room. Finally I'd take them to meet the players and then out onto the pitch. That first time was spine-tingling. I'd been away 13 or 14 years. There had been no announcement on the tannoy. I was in a suit. I had aged. But as I came out on the pitch there was a small ripple of applause from those close up who recognised me. The ripple spread like a trail of gunpowder across the ground as people nudged one another and pointed. Within in a minute or two everyone was up on their feet giving me a standing ovation. My eyes filled up and I nearly broke down as they launched into 'Osgood, Osgood, born is the King of Stamford Bridge.'

One time Huddy popped over to the box where I was chatting to some fans and pulled me aside. 'I've got a problem Ossie,' he whispered 'Mike Kelly says he's going to do me after the game.'

Mike Kelly was a former QPR goalkeeper, here at the Bridge in a coaching role with his team Middlesbrough. He was a large man.

'Why would he want to do that Huddy?'

I can't recall what the reason was now. I'm not sure even Huddy knew, but later I saw Mike near the dressing-rooms. His mood had worsened because his team had just been butchered 5–0 by the Blues. 'What's all this about you're going to do Alan Hudson, Mike?' I asked in a friendly fashion, but I didn't like his attitude when he replied.

'That's right. What's it got to do with you?'

'Well, it's a bit childish, Mike, and you do realise you'll have to go through me first.'

At that I heard someone yell from behind, 'You want some then Kelly?' Suddenly, bodies were rolling around the floor. I dived in to break up the scrapping. To my horror, as luck would have it, the chairman appeared from one direction and Glenn Hoddle, the manager, from the other. Ken Bates, understandably, was furious over the whole incident and with his customary sense of humour called me to his office and said, 'I'm sacking you, Peter, but keeping on Huddy.' When I protested my innocence he started to chuckle and said he'd forgotten the entire incident. He hadn't though, because Alan got the blame and lost the gig.

The chairman could be unnecessarily brutal, I thought. One afternoon Ian Hutchinson came to pick up a couple of complimentary tickets from the office and Ken happened to be around. 'Why is this man receiving complimentary tickets?' he demanded.

'Because he's Ian Hutchinson,' some frightened staff member dared to reply.

Bates told Hutch effectively to get lost and buy a ticket like anyone else. But Hutch wasn't anyone else. He was a great former player who had literally donated his legs to the club. I know chairmen have to draw the line on complimentaries and suchlike (Ken explained to me once the amount of freeloading that was taking place when he first took over), but the situation could have been handled more diplomatically.

Still, no one can detract from the fact that Ken Bates engineered the revival at Stamford Bridge and I was fortunate enough to be there as it all unfolded. Exciting and beautiful football returned, as did League Cups, FA Cups and European Cup-Winners' Cups. Still no championship – but, one day. It has been suggested that some of us old players were not happy about the revival because somehow it took the sheen off our own achievements. Nothing could be further from the truth. It was not the same, as we were not playing and therefore have no 'ownership' of the latest achievements, but as fans it thrilled us no end. Being in Stockholm with Chopper roaring the boys on to win the Cup-Winners' Cup ranks alongside my best nights ever. I love Chelsea and being back there for the last nine years has made my life complete again.

I got to know Matthew Harding, but unfortunately only for a relatively short time. Suddenly I kept hearing his name and eventually someone pointed this young curly-haired bloke out to me. He was wearing jeans and a bit of a pot-belly strained at the buttons of his shirt. 'He's worth zillions,' I was told, 'and he wants to put his dosh into Chelsea.'

We were introduced and he gripped my hand and looked up at me, his eyes dancing. 'The old King, the old King,' he repeated over and over again.

We became pals and I would pop into the Imperial pub before I started work on match days and always have a drink with him, his father and entourage. For a time it seemed a happy development, as Matthew broke down the barriers between the board and the terraces (or seats as they now were) and was willing to put chunks of his substantial fortune into Chelsea. There was a strong rumour that he was going to facilitate Matthew Le Tissier coming from Southampton to Chelsea, but it never came to pass. Sad, because although Matt and the Saints have a mutual love affair, I am sure he was the sort of player that would have hit the stratosphere had he played on the big stage.

I never knew what the deal was with Matthew Harding, Ken Bates and Chelsea Football Club, and have no views on who was right and who was wrong when their relationship deteriorated the way it did. I just thought it was very sad. I was rendered speechless when a journalist rang me one night to break the news that Matthew had died in a helicopter accident returning from an evening Chelsea away game. 'Shall I call you later?' asked the journalist.

I felt a great sense of loss, not so much because we were close – we weren't, we hadn't known each other long enough – but because I felt that he was just at the beginning of what he was going to do. It was such a tragedy for Matthew, his family and friends, and Chelsea Football Club. I mourned for the deep friendship we were going to have.

His widow Ruth asked if I would say a few words at his memorial service a few weeks later and I was honoured to do so. I followed dear old Jimmy Hill and opened up with 'You'll have to forgive Jimmy if he seemed nervous just then, but being associated with Fulham and Coventry most of his life, he's not used to big crowds.' It did the trick and raised a laugh at a very sad time, which is, I'm absolutely sure, what Matthew Harding would have wanted.

I dread and hate these phone calls bearing bad news. I suppose there is no other way really. You're not going to be walking down the High Street and someone stops you and says, 'Oh, by the way, your best pal has died.'

In 1995 I was rung and told that Bobby Stokes had passed away. Dear little Bobby Stokes. We were best mates. He was a lovely, mischievous man who had played with me in the Southampton/Manchester United FA Cup final and assured himself a place in history and the love of the Southampton people forever by scoring that one giant-killing goal. We had worked together again at Portsmouth and always kept in touch. Towards the end of his short life he and Jan, his wife, became close friends of Lynn and me. Even closer than when we were players. I cannot look at a particular picture I have of him and me without welling up. We're in the bath after the 1976 final and Bobby is kissing the trophy, but he has a mildly haunted look on his face, like he's thinking 'Can life really be this good? Where's the catch?' That picture is on the back cover of this book. Look at it and you'll see what I mean.

I always felt that none of us – the town, the team, and myself – had done enough for Bobby and his memory. He is a true hero of Southampton. Last year in 2001, Lynn organised a memorial day for the little man at the Guildhall in Southampton which was attended by 650 people. The day went off well and thanks to Lynn's drive and organisational skills we were able to raise a substantial amount of money and pay for a block of seats at Southampton's stadium to be used for disadvantaged children in Bobby's memory. We all miss him terribly.

Only a couple of years later my tranquillity was interrupted again, although by this time we had entered the world of mobile telephones. A world where people can no longer make themselves inaccessible when they want and we seem to demand instant responses and reactions from one another. 'Alan Hudson has been run over by a car and is unlikely to survive the day.'

My stomach turned over. He had literally been mowed down as he crossed the road in the East End of London where he was now living. His pelvis and legs had exploded, he had serious head injuries and the loss of blood was phenomenal. One of his family told me that the doctors had said that even in the slight chance that he did survive he would be a permanently crippled vegetable. I couldn't get the image out of my mind of the fresh-faced boy who turned up at Stamford Bridge. He was like your kid brother on and off the field then. So eager to learn. So determined to excel. Soaking up every piece of conversation. And he learned so quickly. I have to say, at the risk of offending others, that he was the greatest player I ever played alongside. A wonderful gifted, generous footballer. He has been accused of wasting his talent but that is not true. Others wasted his talent. His debut for England against West Germany was generally agreed to be one of the finest international debuts ever. He was superb, yet he played for England only once again, in a demolition of Cyprus. Not surprisingly as time went by he became increasingly cynical about the game, or more accurately many of the people in it. Many held the same views as Huddy; he was different because he voiced them, and he didn't care to whom.

The vigil around his bedside went from hours to days to weeks. He wasn't getting any better but he just refused to die. The doctors marvelled at his strength and went down on record as saying that never before had they known anyone survive such extensive and serious injuries. One day the blood clot on his brain dissipated and he regained consciousness, and the fears of brain damage proved unfounded. Slowly he began the gargantuan fight for the recovery of his mobility, a fight that continues to this day. Remarkably he has endured scores of operations and hour on hour of painful physiotherapy, but is now walking again and resuming his old life. I can only marvel at his courage and determination.

We're all a bit battered and bruised, us old boys. I have a useless ankle and a knee replaced, and they can tell me a mile off on the golf course by the way I hobble from one hole to the next. Hutch is in a real bad state. As I write he is in hospital battling with liver disease. His partner Elaine is Lynn's old friend who had introduced us to Roland, the comedy scriptwriter. She looks after him well. But this is his biggest battle and we're all praying for his recovery. When I see him in the hospital he gives me that lop-sided smile and I want to throw him over my shoulder and take him home. I want my Hutch back. Chrissy Garland fights Parkinson's disease, but his spirit is undiminished. I'm sure Eddie McCreadie still bears the mental scars from when he caved in under the pressure. And of course we lost Peter Houseman so early on. Is this a sad story? I don't think so. If you take any sample of 20-odd men and revisit them 30 years on I'm sure you'll find a similar catalogue of triumph, tragedy, success and failure. It is real life – that's what it is.

I don't think that any other old team still have as much to do with each other as we do. We are always in touch, not just for official reunions but also in everyday life. We all have fall-outs and we get on each other's nerves from time to time but deep down we all love one another and look out for one another. I'm beginning to sound like a cast member of *Eastenders* now, but it is true.

Lynn Osgood has been my saviour and my inspiration. If we hadn't met up again that day when I was driving to the bank to pay a cheque in, who knows where my life would have gone? I really was at rock bottom. Skint, bankrupt, drinking, aimless. She picked me up, brushed me down and loved me. She presented me with another wonderful son, this time when I was at an age and level of maturity to treasure the childhood years as everyone should. Because boy, does it go fast. She has organised me and enabled me to focus on my assets and contain my liabilities. She has withstood the ups and downs of this roller-coaster life and helped me find perspective. Never has she lost her sense of fun and love of life. I love you Lynn.

In fact I love my life at the moment. I really don't want to die. Not in my lifetime anyway. Getting old is not so bad after all. You tend to worry less about things. See things from a much more relaxed viewpoint. Appreciate the things and people around you. Writing this book brought back many memories, most of them very happy, although even I look back at some of the things we did, cringe and think 'Did I really do that?' I work at my own pace running the golf, the after-dinners and every Saturday doing the hospitality at Chelsea or Southampton. But I have plenty of leisure time when I like to be with my family and friends, and I try to keep in touch with the old boys wherever they are. I love the charity dos because not only do we raise money but it is the nearest thing to playing football – when you're playing you see everyone, every week. The camaraderie and fun is untouchable. Only when it is gone do you realise how good it was. At the charity golf days across the country you meet these people again. We're older now but the eyes and the smiles don't alter. The basic characteristics are the same and for a few hours we're all back there. It's great to see them all, even Emlyn Hughes and the Leeds boys. I want to thank everyone that I know and all those that I don't – those who clicked through the turnstiles to watch me whether at Chelsea, Southampton or anywhere else and made me feel so much part of their lives. It's been a ball.

I never saw him play. I wish I had. All I know is the great love the Chelsea fans have for him. When he comes onto the pitch in his PR capacity there is a real buzz and necks crane across the ground. 'There's Ossie. There's Ossie.'

I. Baddiel, Playwright

EPILOGUE

JULY 2002

Two letters on the mat this morning. I open the first and it is *The Official Chelsea Magazine*. Inside is a poll conducted among former Chelsea players as to who they rate as Chelsea's greatest all-time player. I am amazed and so very proud and flattered that my name is top with 95 votes, nearly a quarter of a century after I kicked my last ball for Chelsea. A couple of years back there was an equivalent poll among readers which I was also delighted to top. Gianfranco Zola, one of the nicest men in the game, was second.

The next envelope is also from Chelsea Football Club. The letter inside is signed by Ken Bates. He tells me that times are hard and that the club is looking to cut its cloth. Thanks for your contribution Peter, but we will not be needing you next season.

I hope Ranieri spends the £10,000 saved wisely.

Que sera sera.

SEPTEMBER 2002

Ian Hutchinson did not recover and sadly died following his long illness. I thank God the big fella has found peace but life can never be quite the same. I dedicate this book to him. See you again bruv.

Appendix

Where Do You Go To, My Lovely?

Jeff Astle returned to the public eye in the 1990s clowning around on the *Baddiel & Skinner* TV show. Sadly he died in 2001.

Tommy Baldwin drives posh cars and looks after foreign dignitaries when they visit London.

Alan Ball had a spell as manager at Manchester City and another stint managing Portsmouth in the 1990s. He is active in organising 1966 World Cup final team events. He lives near me and is one of my best pals.

Roy Bentley is retired and enjoying his golf after spells managing Reading and Swansea. At one point he was secretary of Ron Harris's golf club in Swindon.

George Best is off the sauce and lives happily with his lovely wife Alex deep in the Surrey countryside. He is recovering well from a recent liver transplant.

Alan Birchenall does what he does best – entertaining the crowds as the warm-up man at Leicester City.

Peter Bonetti is still in the game coaching young goalkeepers.

John Boyle works in security. He was my room-mate for many years and I miss his company.

Barry Bridges has a newsagent's shop outside Norwich.

Mike Channon has become a top racehorse trainer. You can sometimes catch him on Channel 4's *The Morning Line*, but you'll be hard pushed to understand a word he says.

Jack Charlton became a successful manager, most notably making Ireland a serious national side. I take back anything unflattering I have said about the big man, because I have just read his autobiography where he says that Alf Ramsey's biggest mistake in Mexico was not playing me against Brazil and West Germany.

Charlie Cooke resides in Cincinnati, USA where he is the director of the Coever Coaching School, a renowned youth soccer-coaching programme.

John Dempsey works with handicapped children.

Kerry Dixon tried desperately to keep Doncaster Rovers above water as manager a few years back. If he gets another chance on the managerial merry-go-round I'm sure he'll do well.

Tommy Docherty is alive and well. His name means 'destroyer' by the way. His forthright opinions are still sought by TV and radio stations across the country. He delivers a mean after-dinner speech too. I recently heard that Tom escaped serious injury when he somehow became entangled in an automatic car wash. This could only have happened to the Doc.

Dick Foss was let go by Tommy Docherty many years ago. He died during the 1990s.

Danny Gillen became a professional minder. Last I heard of him he was looking after Phil Collins.

George Graham famously managed Arsenal during one of their most successful periods but was engulfed by a bungs scandal. Since then he's had spells with Leeds and Tottenham. He'll be back.

Jimmy Greaves was probably the first footballer to 'come out' over alcohol. He has successfully abstained for years now and has enjoyed a prosperous career as a media pundit. For a time the *Saint and Greavsie* show, jointly presented with ex-Liverpool legend Ian St John, enjoyed cult status.

Mick Greenaway died in 1999. Most Chelsea fans never even knew he was ill. A memorial night was held at Stamford Bridge and the money raised funded a headstone that bears the inscription 'True Blue'.

Ron Harris joins me now and then on the after-dinner circuit. He lives in the West Country.

Marvin Hinton drives for a living. He is one of the few people I know that broke his leg *after* he retired from football.

John Hollins managed Chelsea for a while in the 1980s but has recently enjoyed more success with Swansea City. His boy Chris, who is the image of his father at the same age, keeps staring at me from the TV; he works as a sports reporter for the BBC.

Alan Hudson continues to recover from the horrific injuries sustained in his road accident. He is living back in the bosom of his family and friends, a Charlie Cooke chip away from Stamford Bridge.

Emlyn Hughes forged a post-playing career as a panellist on *A Question of Sport* and now works the after-dinner circuit.

Geoff Hurst recently wrote his memoirs and is in much demand in World Cup years, for obvious reasons.

Steve Kember is still at Crystal Palace and as caretaker manager he recently steered them away from relegation.

Joe Kirkup owns and runs a newsagent's shop in Ewell, Surrey. Not sold to him by Ronnie Harris, I hasten to add.

Francis Lee is one of the post-footballing career success stories, making his fortune from bog paper.

Jim McCalliog has a pub in Wetherby. He will not tell me exactly where.

Eddie McCreadie lives in Memphis, USA with his wife. He has now given up hope of getting a company car out of Chelsea Football Club. Recently Alan Hudson visited him and he asked, 'Do they still remember me at the Bridge, Huddy?' Is the Pope a Catholic?

Lawrie McMenemy has managed Sunderland and the Northern Irish national team. He is a motivational and after-dinner speaker.

Bobby Moore died in 1995. One day they will get around to erecting a statue in central London to the only man to captain England to a World Cup final victory. In a drawer at my mum's house is a bracelet he once gave me . . .

Bert Murray runs The Bull public house in Market Deeping near Peterborough. On production of this page, in this book, he will supply you with a free drink.

Robin Nedwell starred in a revival of the Doctor series in the '90s but tragically died following a fall from the roof of his house.

Terry Paine lives in South Africa and is one of their main TV pundits.

Sir Alf Ramsey died in 2000 after many years in the football wilderness. He never really received the permanent appreciation he deserved, but probably didn't want it anyway.

Don Revie died in 1989. His tenure as England manager was short-lived and his true colours were revealed when it was discovered he had told the FA that the job was proving too stressful and asked for a pay-off to 'leave quietly'. He omitted to tell them he had already negotiated a lucrative contract to manage the United Arab Emirates side. The English people effectively shunned him thereafter.

Peter Rodrigues still lives in the Southampton area. No one has told him that moustaches went out with Ford Capris and Betamax videos.

Dave Sexton has scaled the heights in football, having managed Manchester United, and he remains part of the England set up.

Alan Skirton was working the hospitality down at Yeovil Town the last I heard.

Tommy Smith is another who is semi-crippled through injuries sustained in football and the after-effects of being dosed up with cortisone.

Dick Spence carried on watching Chelsea up until his death in 1983.

Jim Steele runs the Black Bear pub in Moreton-in-Marsh.

Bobby Tambling lives happily in Ireland where he coaches a boy's soccer side.

Ian Turner, last I heard, was working on the oilrigs.

Terry Venables keeps rolling along. He's done it all, has Venners, from managing clubs to owning them (one being Portsmouth). He's written books and recorded songs. Somewhere along the line he became England manager. As I write, he has recently become manager of Leeds United. This story is going to run and run.

David Webb is another of the old team to manage Chelsea, even if only for a caretaker period. Still, he acquitted himself well. He remains convinced that one day he will make enough money to buy the club and sack Ken Bates.